Get Creative With
CUBASE VST

Composing and arranging with Cubase VST

Keith Gemmell

PC Publishing

£14·95

PC Publishing
Export House
130 Vale Road
Tonbridge
Kent TN9 1SP
UK

Tel 01732 770893
Fax 01732 770268
email info@pc-publishing.com
web site http://www.pc-publishing.com

First published 2002

© PC Publishing

ISBN 1 870775 75 9

Original music composed by Keith Gemmell, © Music Hot House, all rights reserved.

British Library Cataloguing in Publication Data
A catalogue record for this book is available from the British Library

Printed in Great Britain by Bell and Bain, Glasgow

Preface

Welcome to *Get creative with Cubase VST*. Two questions:

1 Do you want to learn the basics of composition and arranging – the nuts and bolts as it were?
2 Do you also want to learn how to sequence, record and mix your compositions effectively within Cubase VST?

If your answer to those questions is yes, this book will help you do both in a practical and enjoyable way. Nothing stuffy here!

There's an old proverb: *I hear and I forget, I see and I remember, I do and I understand*. That's the essence of this book. Doing the projects and comparing your results along the way to the examples on the CD will provide you with a valuable insight into the creative process. What's more, you will be learning how to use Cubase VST at the same time. Do, and you will understand.

Two things are dealt with here:

1 The creative process – conceiving the ideas and developing them.
2 The production process – capturing, shaping and manipulating those ideas within the Cubase VST environment.

Both elements overlap and this book could just as easily have been entitled *Composing and arranging with Cubase VST*. There's no doubt that much of today's music is produced this way. The most obvious uses are in the pop, techno and dance genres. However these are not the only ones. Cubase VST and similar music software production programs are used to record music for computer games, TV soundtracks, advertising jingles, radio drama and multimedia presentations to name just a few. This book is aimed at helping musicians and students, interested in writing for those kinds of markets, with the composition process; how to get the ideas in the first place and develop, record and mix them into a satisfying whole.

All you need to work through the projects or examine the musical examples on the accompanying CD is the latest version of Cubase VST 5 and a suitable computer and monitor speakers. To participate in the audio recording, a microphone and possibly an external mixer will be needed. However you have the option just to use the supplied audio files. Everything, the sequencing, the audio recording, the effects, dynamic processing and mixing, is done within Cubase itself. The MIDI content makes exclusive use of the VST Instruments supplied with the program including the General MIDI sounds of the Universal Sound Module (USM).

Of course you don't have to actually do the projects if you don't want to. The text can be followed and a great deal learned by just loading and examining the example files.

Very important

Before you 'Get creative', just one thing: Be sure to read the first chapter 'How to use this book and CD'. Reading it will save you time and unnecessary frustration when loading files from the CD.

Contents

How to use this book and CD

Equipment needed

All that's needed, for the projects and examples, is a computer powerful enough to run Cubase VST version 5, equipped with a suitable sound card, a large, fast hard drive and decent monitor speakers.

A typical PC might be: Intel Pentium III or AMD K7, 128 Mb of RAM or more with a large, fast hard drive. Windows 98/ME/2000.

A typical Apple Mac might be: G3 or G4 processor, 128 Mb of RAM or more with a large, fast hard drive. O/S 8.5 or 9.

A high quality, but not necessarily the most expensive, sound card (approved MME or ASIO compliant) is needed. A good, reasonably priced card suitable for both Mac and PC is M/Audio's Audiophile 2496. It features two analogue inputs, two analogue outputs, a break-out cable with S/PDIF input and output plus a MIDI input and output. Other low priced high quality cards are gradually arriving on the market.

A keyboard and MIDI interface will be needed for working through the projects. Some of the projects include audio recording as an option. For this you will need a microphone and possibly an external mixer.

The scheme of things

The book and accompanying CD are integral parts of *Get creative with Cubase VST*. Much of the time you will need to use both along with a copy of Cubase VST 5 running on your computer. This is most certainly the case with the 10 chapters containing projects. Other chapters containing general reading matter also contain references to examples on the CD but make sense away from the computer.

If you already have a working knowledge of Cubase and MIDI sequencing then you may be tempted to skip the first few chapters and projects. That's OK but there is much to be gained, from a musical standpoint, by working through them.

Where possible, for clarity, all Cubase functions are referred to using the program's menus. For example the instruction 'Apply Iterative Quantization' would be followed by the menu command in square brackets: [Functions>Quantizing Type>Iterative]. Power users can speed things up by using the many keyboard shortcuts and alternative methods available. There is usually more than one way of doing things in Cubase VST!

The instruction 'Apply Iterative Quantization'.

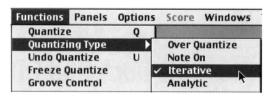

The CD

The CD is compatible with both PC and Apple Mac computers and contains:

- Audio Files supplied in AIF – Audio Interchange File format (with the extension .aif)
- Cubase Song Files (with the extension .all)
- Cubase Arrange Files (with the extension .arr)
- Cubase Part Files (with the extension .prt)
- ReCycle files (with the extension .rex)

INFO

A Song sometimes contains more than one Arrangement. They can be found and opened from the Windows menu [Windows> Arrangements].

These are arranged in folders, relevant to the project or chapter to which they relate. Most chapters refer to musical examples contained on the CD. To examine them, copy the appropriate folder across to your computer desktop or some other location. It is important that all the audio files contained in a folder are copied across and that they remain in their respective folders. Cubase 'remembers' where they are situated and if they are moved problems are likely to arise.

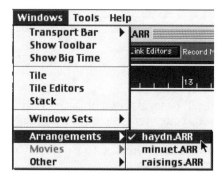

Opening projects containing audio files

From Project 6 onwards you will need to open Cubase song files containing Audio Parts. These files contain the Audio Pool, all audio settings and audio file references. However, they do not contain the actual audio files themselves. Cubase will look for them in their respective folders. When it finds the first audio file a dialogue usually appears to confirm the path for any remaining audio files.

Update your image

Upon opening a Song File fresh from the CD, you may well have to update the Image of the Audio Files before you can see or hear them. Do this in the Audio Pool [Panels>Audio Pool]. In Figure 1.1 the images for the three audio files have yet to be updated and a question mark appears in their place (?). Clicking on the three question marks will update the images (Figure 1.2).

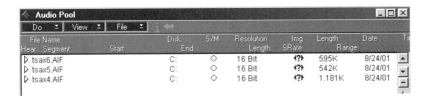

Figure 1.1 In the Audio Pool, the Audio File Images need updating ...

Figure 1.2 ... clicking on the question marks has updated them.

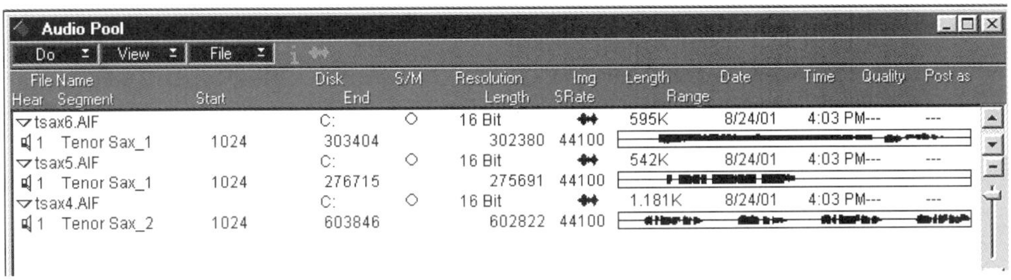

Update the Outputs

When loading a Song file (.all) fresh from the CD, the Universal Sound Module will always be loaded. This can be confirmed by viewing the VST Instrument rack [Panels>VST Instruments]. Any other VST Instruments needed for the Song will also be seen here.

Although the correct Patch Name and Program Numbers will be displayed in the Arrange windows, the Output column – depending on your personal set-up and soundcard – may well display another General MIDI sound source. To hear the Song File as intended, change it to the Universal Sound Module. A few Song Files also use the VST Instruments LM-9 and Neon.

Very important: to ensure that you have the correct Outputs loaded refer to the checklist in the Appendix (page 194) when loading Song Files off the CD.

The projects

The projects are a vital part of *Get Creative with Cubase VST*. Each one builds on the techniques discussed in previous chapters and new Cubase skills are progressively introduced.

Projects 1 – 3 are concerned with MIDI sequencing skills and we record three different styles of music – a rock band, a classical ensemble and a jazz funk band.

Projects 4 – 9 are concerned with composition and arranging. In each one we build a composition from scratch using a predetermined brief. For example, the brief in Project 5 asks us to compose music for a soundtrack using minimalist techniques.

Project 10 is concerned with the business of producing a readable score and parts from the Score and Layout section of Cubase. Here we use a previous project, number 6, as a basis for the work.

All the projects follow a similar pattern and begin with a list of Musical Objectives and Cubase Skills. This is followed by a list of instructions headed Preparation. The first two instructions are always the same. In Project 5, for example:

1 From the CD, copy the folder named 'project5' to your computer. This folder contains all the files you will need for the project. In this case there are 14 Cubase Arrange Files (.arr) and one Cubase Song File (.all).

2 On your computer, create a folder called 'mywork5' or something similar in which to save your work. This is the folder where any work you create will be saved in Cubase Song File format.

This is usually followed by any other general Cubase settings needed such as Tempo and Time Signature.

The last instruction is always something like: In the 'mywork5' folder, save as Song File – myproj5.all – or something similar.

Next comes the Brief which contains an imaginary commission and scenario for the project. For example the Brief for Project 5 begins like this:

OK, here's the scenario. A computer game company has commissioned you to compose the music for a scene in their latest historical title set in Elizabethan times. The piece must run for a minimum of 3 minutes...

Each project contains a series of 'takes.' This is usually an instruction to record something in Cubase. At the beginning of each take is a list of settings to make in the Arrange window. For example Project 5, Take 1 looks like Figure 1.3.

Figure 1.3 Project 5, Take 1 – Settings.

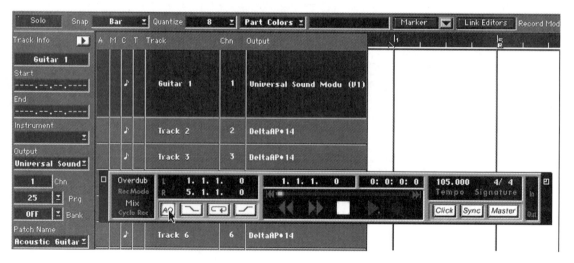

Take 1

• Select Track 1 (Ch 1) and rename it 'Guitar 1'

Track Inspector
Output: USM
Program: 25
Patchname: Acoustic Guitar

Status Bar
Quantize [8]

Transport Bar
(L) 1.1.1 (R) 5.1.1
Activate AQ

The first line tells us which Track to select, its Channel setting and a name for the Track. Next come the Track Inspector settings for this Track. The Output refers to the sound source. In this case it is the Universal Sound Module (USM) and is loaded by selecting [Panels>VST Instruments]. The Program number and Patchname tell us which General MIDI instrument to select.

The Status Bar settings come next. This is usually restricted to just the Quantize value. Sometimes a Snap value is indicated.

Last are the Transport Bar settings needed for the take. The Locator settings are always indicated plus any other relevant information for the Take such as a Tempo change. In this case we are told to activate the AQ (Automatic Quantize) button.

We then follow the text and perform the Take itself. At the completion of a take there is always an instruction to save the work. In Project 5 it is:

Save song – compare with project5/1.arr.

At this point you:

1 Save your work as a Song File – mywork5/myproj5.all
2 Compare it with the example Arrange file (1.arr) in the project 5 folder copied over from the CD. It will not sound exactly the same as yours because you will have played it differently. However, it should be something similar. If you are happy with the result then close down the example Arrange File and continue with the project.

Each time a take is completed, follow the same procedure and save your work as a Song File. The comparison Arrange File will always correspond to where you are in the project. If your version has gone astray in some way, you can always continue by working on the example instead. However, to avoid confusion, if you are happy with the result of your work it is best to close down the example Arrange File.

Of course you do not have to actually do the projects if you don't want to. The text can be followed and much learned by just loading and examining the example files.

VST Instruments used

All of the MIDI content in the example Cubase Files utilises the VST Instruments supplied with the program. This allows you to hear everything exactly as intended. For example, Chapter 5 – 'Get real with MIDI Part 2' – contains the following:

'Here are two interpretations of a short flute solo. Load realism/flutes/flutes.all'

The Song File will be loaded complete with the Universal Sound Module and flute patch (prg.74). Although the USM itself is loaded, the Output, in the Track Inspector or Output column may need updating. Another sound source can be substituted for the USM if desired. It will not, of course, sound the same. In this particular case it will not matter, because only one instrument is used.

For scores containing several instruments it is best to keep to the USM, otherwise things will very likely sound unbalanced. A check-list can be found in the Appendix to this book. If your copy of Cubase does not contain the USM you will have to use another sound source or upgrade to the latest version.

The Universal Sound Module (USM)

The Universal Sound Module (Figure 1.4) is a General MIDI compatible sound module and is used extensively in the projects and musical examples. General MIDI (GM) defines a standardized group of sounds for compatible synthesizers and sound modules. Whatever the program number sent, a GM instrument will always play the correct sound type. The problem is, the quality and detail of these sounds can vary enormously from one manufacturer to another. As a consequence, Song

Figure 1.4 The Universal Sound Module.

Files created using say GM module A can sound very different played back on GM module B.

The problem is solved by the Universal Sound Module. Cubase users can now play files created on computers other than their own confident in the knowledge that things will sound correct. Perfect for the *Get creative with Cubase VST* projects and examples.

The USM also features four stereo outputs. This is particularly useful for routing sounds to different Send Effects processors in the VST Channel Mixer. For detailed information refer to the Cubase documentation.

Figure 1.5 The VST Performance window.

Other VST Instruments used are the LM-9 drum machine and the Neon synthesizer.

VST Plug-ins used

Because the projects and musical examples will be used on various computers with widely differing processing power, extensive use of VST Send Effects has been avoided. No more than two Send Effects are usually operating at any given time. The same applies to the VST Dynamic processors and EQ.

You can monitor the processing power being used in the VST Performance window [Panels>VST Performance] (Figure 1.5) and if you experience problems, disable the least important Send Effect or Dynamic processors currently in use.

Figure 1.6.Reverb effect.

Reverb is the most commonly used Send Effect when mixing the projects (Figure 1.6). Pre-sets are generally used as a starting point. Other Send Effects are used such as DoubleDelay and Chorus.

EQ (Figure 1.7) and VST Dynamics (Figure 1.8) are used in various projects where appropriate.

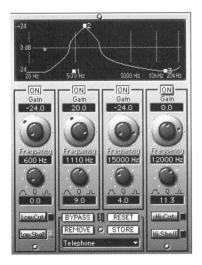

Figure 1.7 EQ.

Figure 1.8 Dynamics.

OK, that's it. Let's Get Creative.

2

MIDI sequencing – make it easy on yourself

A myth dispelled

Freddie is frustrated. For over an hour, as part of a college assignment, he's been slaving away on his MIDI keyboard, attempting to record a piano part into Cubase VST. Trouble is, Fred's main instrument is guitar and although he has a basic knowledge of reading music, his keyboard skills leave a lot to be desired. The piece is only eight measures long and in a simple rock style but each time he does a 'take' there is always something wrong. Sometimes it's out of time, other times it contains bum notes. 'I could be here all day', he thinks, 'and still not get it right.'

I know how he feels. It's a common myth that you have to be a good keyboard player to succeed at arranging and composing. My main instruments are clarinet and saxophone, and I too, am a 'technically challenged' piano player! However, I do manage to write a great deal of music despite my lack of technique. It was a problem until powerful sequencer programs like Cubase VST appeared on the scene. Now I can actually play the music I write! You can do the same. Here are a few pointers, but first an analogy.

Freddie is practising a transcribed guitar solo and encounters a difficult passage containing some awkward licks. What does he do? No, he doesn't give up and play a 12 bar blues instead! He slows the tempo down to a manageable speed, homes in on the nasty bits, and practises those parts repeatedly until he can play them properly. He then puts it all together again, increases the speed and performs a blistering solo. Well that's the theory anyway!

We can apply these principles to the sequencing of piano, or for that matter, any other instrument within Cubase VST.

Slow it down

If you can't play it then slow it down. Why struggle? Computers don't make everything in life easy (the opposite is often the case) but they certainly help us dodgy piano players! However, there is a drawback to playing at a slow tempo, and that's accuracy of timing. Fortunately Quantization comes to the rescue if that's a problem. More on this in a moment.

Let's suppose you are recording a piece with Cubase at 120 bpm. and you come up against a passage that you can't play at that speed. Open the Mastertrack [Edit>List>Mastertrack] and if not already set – 120bpm is the default setting – change it to 120 bpm (Figure 2.1).

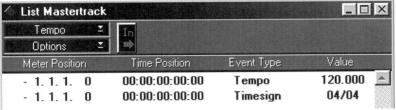

Figure 2.1 The List Mastertrack – default settings.

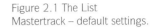

Figure 2.1a Uncheck Tempo/Mute Recording.

Ensure that Tempo/Mute Recording is unchecked [Options>Record Tempo/Mute] (Figure 2.1a).

In the Transport Bar, slow the Tempo to something more comfortable like 80bpm (Figure 2.2).

Set the Locators accordingly and record the tricky bit. To hear the result at the correct speed (120 bpm), all you have to do is click on the Master button (just below the Tempo display) and the playback switches to 120 bpm (Figure 2.3).

If you're happy with it, deactivate the Master switch and continue recording at any tempo you like. The Mastertrack has stored the original tempo. It will not change until you edit it.

Figure 2.2 Slow the Tempo to 80 bpm ...

Figure 2.3 ...activate the Master button to return to 120 bpm.

TIP

*W*hen the Tempo/Mute Recording option is checked you run the risk of accidentally recording your tempo changes into the Mastertrack. Check this only when you require permanent tempo alterations.

Break it down

This is very important. Why play large chunks of music and get it repeatedly wrong? Make good use of all this technology. Break the music down into manageable chunks. An eight measure section can very easily be recorded in two four measure sections, or even smaller sections. It is important though, particularly if the material is melodic, to identify phrases, and record them intact where possible. This will help you avoid any loss of continuity and 'feel' that may occur through recording this way.

If the music is of a rhythmic character you will probably be able to break things down into significantly smaller segments. Only where necessary of course. Don't overdo it and actually increase your working time. The main purpose of all this is to get things done quickly and easily.

Cycle record

One of the most useful things about recording in Cubase VST is the Cycle Record Mode activated by the button on the Transport Bar (Figure 2.4). The ability to continuously repeat a tricky part and overdub piece by piece inside the cycle, adding more music on each lap is invaluable. Again this is akin to the way we practise difficult sections on our instruments. The cycle is set up within the Left and Right Locator positions.

Figure 2.4 The Cycle Record button.

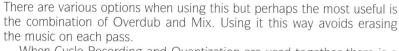

TIP

*W*hen recording in Cycle mode, press the mouse button over the text 'Cycle Rec'. A pop-up menu appears with several editing functions.

There are various options when using this but perhaps the most useful is the combination of Overdub and Mix. Using it this way avoids erasing the music on each pass.

When Cycle Recording and Quantization are used together there is a danger of Double Notes caused by recording events twice. These not only sound strange but can cause problems on some synthesizers. Fortunately, they can be easily erased [Functions>MIDI Functions> Delete Doubles] (Figure 2.4a).

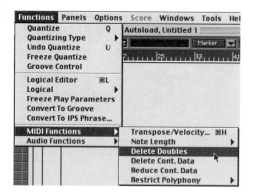

Figure 2.4a Double notes are easily erased using 'Delete Doubles'.

To quantize or not to quantize

TIP

A quick way to quantize is to record with the AQ button activated on the Transport Bar.

Figure 2.5.The AQ button (Automatic Quantize).

Musicians argue endlessly over this. There's no doubt that quantization helps tremendously to tighten up loosely played performances. On the other hand it can render a beautifully expressive performance completely lifeless. So when do we resort to quantization? Well, let's suppose you are composing techno music as background music for a science documentary video. In this case quantization is probably a must. Computer music by its very nature lends itself to this kind of treatment. On the other hand, if you were working on music of a romantic nature, for a chocolate box selection advert, the music would need to 'breathe' in a rubato fashion. In this case quantization would be used sparingly, if at all.

Those are two extremes and there are many styles of music and combinations of instruments which fall in between. Choices have to be made.

Editing – get rid of the bum notes!

We all make mistakes and one of the beauties of Cubase VST is the ability to edit any mistakes and wrong notes after recording. If you've followed the principles outlined above, hopefully, there will not be too many.

If you are familiar with conventional music notation you will find it easiest to alter, delete, and replace wrong notes in the Score Editor. [Edit>Score] (Figure 2.6). If not, you may prefer the Key Editor [Edit>Edit] where you will find a graphic representation of the recording with the notes placed on a grid (Figure 2.7). It's easy to determine the pitch from the virtual keyboard on the left hand side. For detailed use of these Editors, refer to your Cubase manual.

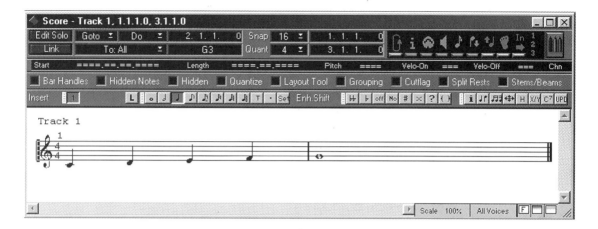

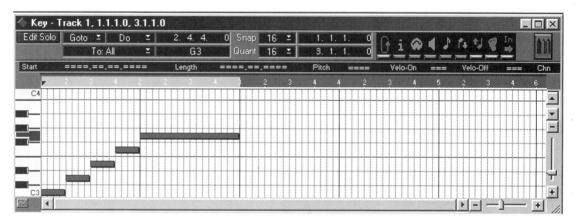

Ok, enough talking. Let's do it. In the next chapter, by recording a simple rock and roll piano score we will become familiar with the basic techniques of sequencing and some of the most frequently used functions and tools within Cubase VST.

Above: Figure 2.6 The Score Editor.

Below: Figure 2.7 The Key Editor.

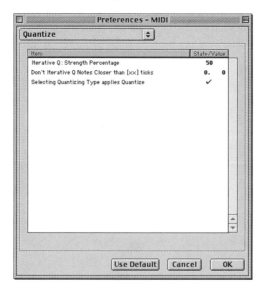

3

Project 1 – some rock 'n' roll piano

Musical objectives
- Record a simple rock 'n roll piano part; length 8 measures.

Cubase skills
- Set a Master Tempo in the Mastertrack.
- Toggle between the Master Tempo and a suggested user tempo for ease of playing.
- Apply Iterative Quantization.

Preparation
- From the CD, copy the folder 'project1' to your computer.
- On your computer, create a folder called 'mywork1' or something similar in which to save your work.
- Prepare an Arrange window containing two MIDI Tracks and corresponding Channels.
- On the Transport Bar, set the Time Signature to 4/4.
- Go to the Quantize dialogue box. [Edit>Preferences> MIDI>Quantize] and select the Default setting (Figure 3.1).

Figure 3.1 The Quantize dialogue box.

- Our tempo for this piece is 100bpm. Set this in the Mastertrack. [Edit>List Mastertrack] Scroll the tempo to 100. The Timesign will show 4/4 if it has already been set on the Transport Bar. Close the Mastertrack Editor and scroll the Tempo on the Transport Bar to a suitable number. I have chosen 90 bpm. You may prefer something slower.
- In the 'mywork1' folder, save as Song File – myproj1.all – or something similar.

Before you start, have a listen to project1/project1.all on the CD and view the score (Figure 3.2). This will help those of you still developing your music reading skills to get the gist of it.

Figure 3.2 Rock 'n' roll piano score

Remember to set the Output column to the VST Instrument called Universal Sound Module first, otherwise you may not hear anything.

Ensure the Output columns display the USM.

Take 1

- Select Track 2 (Ch 2) and rename it 'Left Hand'.

Track Inspector
Output: USM
Program: 1
Patch Name: Acoustic Grand Piano

Status Bar
Quantize [8]

Transport Bar
Locators: (L) Left 1.1.1. (R) 5.1.1

Figure 3.3 Record the first
four bars of the left hand
piano part.

- Record the first four bars of the left hand part (Figures 3.3 and 3.4).

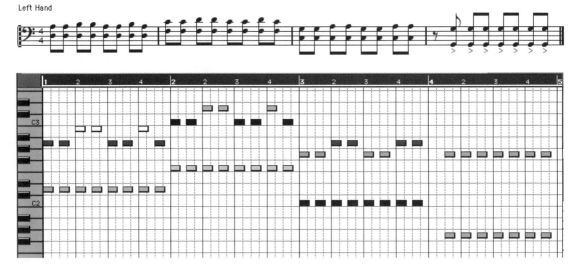

Figure 3.4 The first four bars
of the left hand piano part
(Key Edit view)

You don't have to use your left hand only. This is not a piano lesson!
Use both hands if it makes it easier. I do.

> ### TIP
>
> *You may prefer to load project1/project1.arr from the CD first and listen
> through before you begin recording.*

Listen back. Our Quantize value has been set to 8. Selecting the Part
you have just recorded and choosing Over Quantize followed by
Quantize will move every note you played to the nearest 8th note. This
will sound fine. However, rock 'n roll piano is often just a little loose. I
have used Iterative Quantize on mine.

This type of Quantizing moves the notes towards the closest Quantize value, if they are not already very close. How much the notes are moved, and what is considered 'already close to the Quantize value', is set using the 'Strength' and 'Don't Q' parameters in the Quantize dialogue box. We used a 'Strength' of 50% and left the 'Don't Q' option at 0 (default setting) (Figure 3.1).

Figure 3.5 Activate the Master Button to listen at the correct tempo.

- Activate the Master button on the Transport Bar (Figure 3.5) to listen at the correct tempo. If it's not as tight as you would like apply Quantization again.

- Save song – compare with project1/1.arr.

When loading *my* Cubase Arrange files into *your* Song file version for comparison, remember to:

1 Check that the Universal Sound Module has been loaded.
2 Ensure the Output columns display the USM.
3 To avoid confusion, close down *my* Arrange file version before any further saving of *your* Song file.

TIP

A *quick way to apply Quantization – select a Part and press Q on your computer keyboard.*

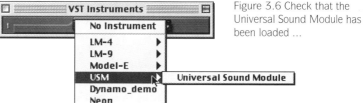

Figure 3.6 Check that the Universal Sound Module has been loaded ...

... and ensure the Output columns display the USM.

Take 2

- Select Track 1 (Ch 1) and rename it 'Right Hand'.

Track Inspector
Output: USM
Program: 1
Patch Name: Acoustic Grand Piano

Status Bar
Quantize [8]

Transport Bar
Locators: (L) Left 1.1.1. (R) 5.1.1

- Deactivate the Master button on the Transport Bar and reset to your preferred tempo.
- Now record the first four bars of the right hand piano part (Figures 3.7 and 3.8). If it is difficult to play, try playing the two harmonies separately on different passes.
- Listen back and, if necessary, apply Iterative Quantization.

Figure 3.7 Record the first four bars of the right hand piano part.

Figure 3.8 The first four bars of the right hand piano part (Key Edit view).

I expect you have noticed that bars 5, 6, and 7 in the left hand part are the same as bars 1, 2 and 3 (Figure 3.2). To save time (and possibly high blood pressure, depending on your piano playing skills) we'll copy those bars to bar 5.

- With the Song Position Pointer at 4.1.1 use the Scissors Tool to split the Part (Figure 3.8a).
- Select the first 3 bars (1 – 4) and copy and paste to bar 5. Alternatively, select the first 3 bars (1 – 4) and duplicate the new Part to bar 5 by dragging it. (Click, hold and drag while pressing Alternate (Mac: Option) on your computer keyboard).

Figure 3.8a Use the Scissors Tool to split the Part

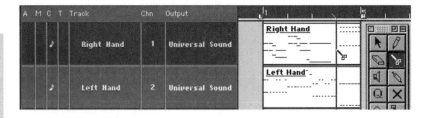

TIP

When pasting a copied Part, make sure the Song Position Pointer is set to the exact destination otherwise the Part will be pasted somewhere else!

The right hand part follows the same pattern so repeat the above procedure on that Part too.

- Save song – compare with project1/2.arr.

Take 3

- Return to Track 2, set the Locators between 8.1.1 and 9.1.1 and record the last bar of the left hand piano part (Figures 3.9 and 3.10).
- Switch to Track 1 and record the last bar of the right hand piano part (Figures 3.11 and 3.12). If necessary, apply Iterative Quantize to both and you're done.

Left Hand

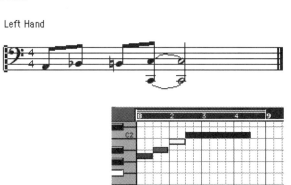

Figure 3.9 Record the last bar of the left hand piano part.

Figure 3.10 The last bar of the left hand piano part viewed in Key Edit.

Right Hand

Figure 3.11 Record the last bar of the right hand piano part.

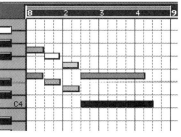

Figure 3.12 The last bar of the right hand piano part seen in the Key Edit window.

- Save song – compare with project1/3.arr.

4

Get real with MIDI – part 1

As part of a college assignment, Sara has been sequencing classical music, a string quartet, with Cubase VST. She has played all the parts correctly from her MIDI keyboard, but for some reason, the overall result is less than convincing. The instruments just don't sound realistic.

This is a common scenario. Of course it's well nigh impossible to recreate the performance of a real violinist, or come to that, any other instrumentalist, but a pretty convincing job can be made of it if we approach things the right way. We may not be able to fool musicians, but we can certainly produce something worthy enough for many a multimedia project. However, there is much to learn to achieve a good result.

Use your imagination

So how do we transform our Cubase VST projects into sounding like the London Philharmonic Orchestra or, for that matter, Led Zeppelin? By using our imagination, of course. Whether you have a top of the range sound card, or just a humble Sound Blaster Live card, you will not get far without it.

Forget the keyboard and concentrate on the virtual instrument you are recording. If it's a violin, imagine yourself actually playing it. Be that violinist. You are bowing those short rhythmic stop notes, those long flowing melodies that string sections are so good at. The same applies to any instrument. Try to get inside the mind of your virtual musician. Before you can do this confidently, you will have to spend time listening.

Listen and learn

Listen to all kinds of music. To earn a crust, arrangers and composers must be able to write in just about any style. If you can afford it, get out and attend live music events and hear as much variation of style as possible. Classical – old and contemporary – jazz, rock, folk, in fact just about anything. These day's there's a wealth of recorded material available on the Internet in all styles, old and new. Select the good stuff and download it. You don't have to like all this music but you should absorb it. It will all resurface when you need it.

Learn how to listen

There's not much point in listening to all this music if you haven't learned how to listen. Instead of just listening to the overall sound picture, train your ear to single out the instruments from orchestras, groups and bands. Identify the musical families they belong to.

Was that an oboe or a cor Anglais solo? Is that a viola or violin playing those low notes? Is he playing a fretless bass guitar or just a regular electric bass guitar on that ballad? Are those trombones or French horns in that quiet orchestral passage? Is that a tenor or alto saxophone break in that jazz rock number?

These are the kinds of questions you should ask yourself. This is easy in a live situation, but considerably harder with recorded music. Pay particular attention to the way these instruments are played, both in a solo situation and as part of a section. It's also important to understand the comfortable playing range of the various instruments.

Get a life – play with others!

Working with Cubase VST provides a wonderful virtual environment, but unfortunately it's usually a solitary one. As well as listening, there is no substitute for actually playing live, in rock bands, jazz bands, wind bands, orchestras, folk groups and so on. The list is endless. This provides invaluable first hand experience of how real instruments are played. If you can, have a go at some of these instruments (ask first of course).

5

Get real with MIDI – part 2

To examine the Cubase files for this chapter, from the CD, copy the folder named 'realism' to your computer.

I mentioned earlier how important it is to use our imagination when playing what are, after all, imaginary instruments. OK they are samples of real instruments, but lifeless unless we know how to use them. Here are some pointers.

Sequencing woodwinds and brass

The woodwinds, in the main, are split into two groups, reed instruments – clarinets, oboe, cor Anglais (English horn), bassoons, saxophones – and flutes, recorders and piccolos.

The brass are comprised mainly of trumpets, trombones, horns, and tuba. Here are the key points to remember:

Woodwind and brass players need to breathe! I've heard many a woodwind part ruined by a virtuoso keyboard player who has not thought about this.

Be careful not to create overlaps when playing from the keyboard. If it happens (Figure 5.1) then clean them up with Functions>MIDI Functions>Note Length>Del. Overlaps (poly/mono) (Figure 5.2).

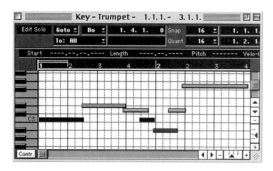

Figure 5.1 Before – overlapping trumpet notes.

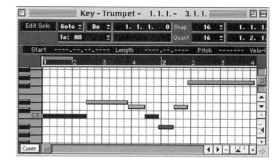

Figure 5.2 After – Del Overlaps/poly applied.

Bear in mind that 'blowers' articulate with their tongues. Unless a passage is deliberately slurred there should be small gaps between notes. This is sometimes difficult to achieve and a bit of a fiddle but it's usually a matter of keeping the best take and polishing it up afterwards, in either the Score or Key Editors.

Here are two interpretations of a short flute solo.

- Load realism/flutes.all (Figure 5.3).
- Set the Output column to the Universal Sound Module.

Mozart Symphony No.40 flute.arr

Figure 5.3 Mozart Symphony No.40 – flutes.all.

This Song File contains two Arrangements. The first – flutes/badflt.arr – is badly played and ignores the breath mark (V) in the fourth measure. The second – flutes/goodflt.arr – pays heed to the articulation and has a gap for that all important breath.

Saxophone solos will require subtle use of pitch bend to make them sound at all convincing. This is best done whilst playing, using the pitch bend controller on the MIDI keyboard. Pitch bend can be added afterwards but it's hard to beat the spontaneity of adding it live. Here's an example.

- Load realism/alto/hodges.all.
- Set the Output column to the Universal Sound Module.

This is a short solo in the style of the late Johnny Hodges, famed for his beautiful tone and incredible note bending. Well I can't guarantee the tone – this is a synthetic sax after all! – but I have managed to emulate his playing style with the use of pitch bend.

You can inspect the pitch bend (and modulation) in the List Editor [Edit>List] as a graphic representation on the right of the screen and as numerical information on the left (Figure 5.4).

Figure 5.4 Pitch bend data, viewed in the List Edit window.

Start-Pos	Length	Val.1	Val.2	Val.3	Event Type
1. 3. 2.120	3. 2.1760	G4	83	64	Note
1. 3. 2.1440	====.==.====	63	37	===	Pitch Bend
1. 3. 2.2080	====.==.====	11	29	===	Pitch Bend
1. 3. 3.1760	====.==.====	94	29	===	Pitch Bend
1. 3. 3.2400	====.==.====	3	31	===	Pitch Bend
1. 3. 4.1120	====.==.====	41	32	===	Pitch Bend
1. 3. 4.2080	====.==.====	33	34	===	Pitch Bend
1. 3. 4.2720	====.==.====	108	36	===	Pitch Bend
1. 3. 4.3360	====.==.====	100	38	===	Pitch Bend
1. 4. 1. 160	====.==.====	55	39	===	Pitch Bend
1. 4. 1.1760	====.==.====	10	40	===	Pitch Bend
1. 4. 1.2880	====.==.====	47	41	===	Pitch Bend
1. 4. 1.3520	====.==.====	2	42	===	Pitch Bend
1. 4. 2. 640	====.==.====	39	43	===	Pitch Bend
1. 4. 2.1280	====.==.====	122	43	===	Pitch Bend
1. 4. 2.2240	====.==.====	77	44	===	Pitch Bend

List - Alto Sax, 1.1.1.0, 9.1.1.0
Edit Solo | Goto | Do | 1. 1. 4. | 0 | Snap | 16 | 1. 1. 1. | 0
Mask | To: All | Ins. Note | Quant | 16 | 3. 1. 1. | 0

Figure 5.4a Click on the button below the keyboard ...

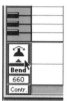

Figure 5.4b ... an icon appears.

Figure 5.5 Pitch bend data, viewed in the Key Edit window.

Another way to view the pitch bend information is in the Key Editor [Edit>Edit]. Click on the button (Figure 5.4a) just below the keyboard, on the lower, left side of the screen. An icon appears (Figure 5.4b). Click this to select pitch bend, or any other controller, from the pop-up menu and a graphic representation appears in the lower half of the screen.

Pitch bend can be drawn and edited from here using the Pencil Tool whilst holding down Alt (Mac: Option) on your computer keyboard to draw in the information (Figure 5.5).

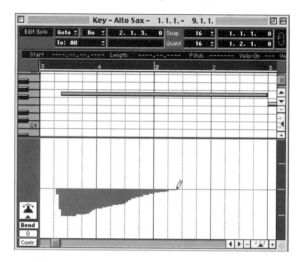

Yet another way of editing pitch bend is in the Controller Editor [Edit>Controller] (Figure 5.6). As with the Key Editor, use the Pencil Tool draw in the information.

Figure 5.6 Pitch bend data, viewed in the Controller Edit window.

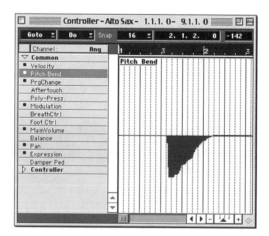

Sequencing strings

The conventional string orchestra uses four instruments. The violin, viola, cello and bass. Here are some key points to remember:

- Distinguish between legato playing (long bowed sections) and individually bowed notes.
- As with the wind instruments, small gaps between individual notes are best, so try to adapt your playing style for this.
- To emulate those long flowing lines it's probably best to select the notes required and apply Legato [Functions>MIDI Functions>Note Length>Legato]. A dialogue box appears where you can set a Legato overlap. A setting of 0.00 is fine.

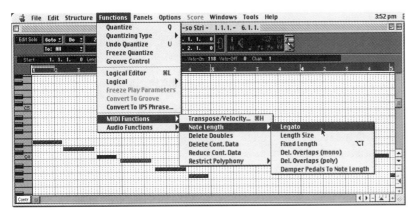

Select the required notes and apply Legato...

... then Set the Legato overlap in the dialogue box.

- A higher setting is usually best avoided, particularly if the notes are at the same pitch. However, a setting just a little under is OK, –0.40 for example, works just fine.

Here's an example (Figure 5.7):

Figure 5.7 Legato strings

- Load realism/strings/strings.all.
- Set the Output column to the Universal Sound Module.

This Song File contains two Arrange Files. The first – okstrngs.arr – has been played accurately enough, but the legato phrases remain choppy.

In the second – lgstrngs.arr – Legato has been applied. All the notes line up end to end and the result is more authentic sounding. Check them in the Key Editor.

If you are using a GM sound source, use Strings 1 for general section work but consider using Strings 2 – sometimes called 'Slow Strings' – for long sustained notes and very slow moving passages.

TIP

String players can play longer lines than wind players because they don't pause for breath – but their arms can ache. Give 'em a break sometimes!

Sequencing drums and percussion

Many Cubase VST users prefer to sequence their drum parts by entering the beats in the Drum Editor. This is fine for music that relies heavily on drum loops, such as dance music. Others prefer to play a 'virtual kit'. It depends on the style of music. If dynamic variation and a live feel is required it's probably best to play the part first and edit it afterwards in one of the Editors. If a repetitive loop is needed, step entry may be the way to go.

Another myth; 'Drums underpin the track so we have to record them first'. Not so. Unless the music is loop based – in which case they will probably be entered step by step anyway – it's often best to record some melodic material first. The advantage of this is that you will be playing with the other parts. All the dynamic variation and feel of the other parts will influence how you play the 'virtual drum kit' and will help instill 'feel' into the music.

For 'live style drums,' here are a few pointers:

• If possible record in stretches of eight bars or so at a time. This helps create a natural flow and is preferable to cutting and pasting one or two bar segments.
• Drum rolls are often best sequenced by mouse entry. It's no easy matter to roll two fingers as fast as two drum sticks. This is usually done in the Drum Editor.
• On a conventional kit try playing the kick and snare drums first and overdub the hi-hats, cymbals and toms afterwards on separate Tracks.

To illustrate how this might be done, I've recorded a four bar rock groove with a fill in the fourth bar. It was done in three stages.

• I laid down the kick drum and snare together for three bars and left the fourth bar blank. Drums are perhaps the hardest instrument to play accurately from a MIDI keyboard – that's my excuse anyway – so I set Quantize at 16 and used the Iterative Quantize function to tighten them up.
• I moved to a different Track, and added the hi-hat figure again using the Iterative Quantize function.
• I then moved to a third Track and recorded the fill on toms with a cymbal crash thrown in for good measure.

Having the drums separated like this also makes it easier to carry out editing procedures.

• Load realism/drums/groove.all.
• Set the Output columns to the Universal Sound Module and listen to the result (extended to eight bars).
• Examine the Parts in the Drum, Key and Score Editors (Figures 5.8, 5.8a and 5.8b).
• Select all the Parts for an overall picture. Check that the General MIDI Drum Map is loaded to view the score [File>Open from Library>General MIDI Drum Map].

TIP

*A*void playing three things on the same beat – apart from the Kick Drum – because drummers don't have three arms and it may sound unnatural!

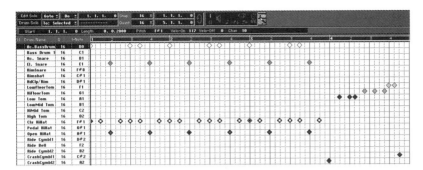

Figure 5.8 Drums – groove.all – viewed in the Drum Edit window.

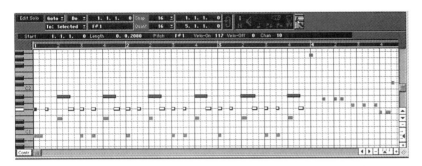

Figure 5.8a Drums – groove.all – viewed in the Key Edit window.

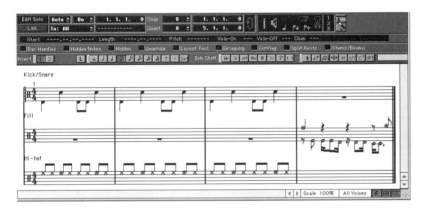

Figure 5.8b Drums – groove.all – viewed in the Score Edit window.

Sequencing guitars

How we approach this depends on whether the instrument is acoustic or electric and whether the music is melodic or rhythmic. Straightforward melodic lines are quite easy with nylon string, steel string and jazz guitars but judicious use of pitch bend will often be needed.

Rock guitar lines are harder. More pitch bend is usually required. Modulation can be added afterwards on a separate Track and is one way to simulate a real players use of vibrato. Take care not to overdo it though.

• Load realism/gtr/lick.all to hear a short lick recorded this way.
• Set the Output column to the Universal Sound Module.

Figure 5.9 Modulation data viewed in the Controller Edit window.

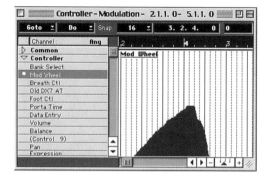

Use the Controller, List and Key Editors to examine the pitch bend and modulation information. The Controller Editor in Figure 5.9 shows the modulation on Track 2.

If Options>Part Appearance>Show Events is checked, the Controller Events will appear on the actual Parts themselves (Figure 5.10).

Figure 5.10 Parts with 'Show Events' checked.

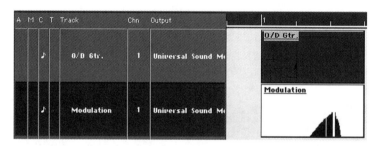

Rhythm guitars need to be approached carefully. Although a real guitar has six strings, things can get very muddy if we try to faithfully reproduce this with a synthesized MIDI guitar. We will also use up valuable polyphony, and on a busy sequence this could result in the unexpected drop out of notes on other instruments.

Try using less notes in a chord. Real guitarists do not always use all six strings anyway. Often three notes are all that is needed if the guitar is used in the background. Open spacing can give the illusion of depth. For example, a chord of C major – C3, E3, G3 (Figure 5.11) could be played as G2, E3, C4.

Figure 5.11 Open spacing can provide depth.

Close voicing   Open voicing

'But what about seventh chords' I hear you say. Omit the fifth or the root but keep the third. How you move from chord to chord depends very much on voice leading and is a vast subject beyond the scope of this book.

Guitar players can of course use a special MIDI interface to play in their parts. This could be useful for playing bass, string and horn parts and other monophonic instruments, but the guitar itself would be best recorded on an Audio Track within Cubase VST.

Quantization

Cubase VST provides plenty of choice here. Which option you choose depends mainly on the instrument you are imitating and the style of music. The two most useful options for everyday sequencing are Over Quantize and Iterative Quantize.

Choosing 'Over Quantize' will move all the notes played to the nearest division of the beat. Selecting 8 in the Quantize value box on the Status Bar will move things to the nearest 8th note, 16 to the nearest 16th note and so on.

Choosing 'Iterative Quantize' will give a less rigid result. Notes are moved towards the Quantize value according to a percentage value. (50% moves them half way). You can also specify a 'window' within which notes will not be Quantized.

When and how much to Quantize depends mainly on the musical material being sequenced. For example, you may be recording a flowing string melody. In this case Quantization is best avoided. However if it's a rhythmic 'marcato' string part then some Quantization may be appropriate. After all real string players are often behind the beat. Only joking!

Here's an example. A three piece horn section – trumpet, tenor saxophone and baritone saxophone – recorded as MIDI instruments into Cubase VST can be very accurately played but somehow still sound imprecise when recorded without Quantization.

- Load realism/horns/horns.all.
- Set the Output columns to the Universal Sound Module.

There are three Arrangements included in this Song File. Have a listen to horns.arr. What do you think? Examine the Parts in the Score Editor and you will see that they are all played accurately enough. What do I think? OK I suppose, but I'd want better than that if was hiring them! View the Parts in the Key Edit and things don't look so tight.

If the Over Quantize option is used or the Automatic Quantize button on the Transport Bar is activated whilst recording things are very much improved because the actual note lengths are left unchanged but they all start at exactly the same time. This retains the sense of 'realness' and is close to how a brass section actually plays. In fact we have achieved exactly what most 'real' horn sections strive for!

Listen to hornsqua.arr. Much tighter, but now they lack feeling and sound a bit mechanical. A quick way to loosen things up without spoiling the tight feel would be to randomize the notes by a few ticks.

A similar effect can be achieved by applying Iterative Quantize to a recorded Part. Depending on how this is set up, only certain notes are moved. It can be progressively applied until the required degree of tightness is heard.

Listen to hornsit.arr. That's more like it. The cheques are in the post!

Dynamics

A fine musical performance, whatever the genre, usually contains a degree of dynamic variation. It goes without saying that a MIDI sequence that emulates such a performance must also contain the same dynamic ingredients; volume (loud or soft) gradual changes of volume (crescendo and diminuendo) sudden changes of volume (sforzando) and accented notes. Three MIDI controllers are used dynamically in Cubase VST: volume, expression and velocity.

Velocity controls the volume of an individual note depending on how hard or soft a key is struck on your MIDI keyboard. Again imagination is needed. Be that percussionist. Take this timpani figure for example (Figure 5.12).

Figure 5.12 A timpani figure – timpani.all.

• Load realism/timpani/timpani.all.
• Set the Output column to the Universal Sound Module.

Listen and examine the Part in the Controller Editor (Figure 5.13). You will notice that the Velocity values start at 55 and end at 125. The gradual increase in attack is not exact, nor would it be if played by a real percussionist.

Figure 5.13 timpani.all – the velocity data viewed in the Controller Edit window.

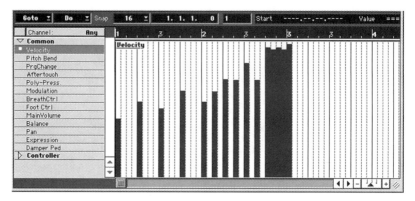

Volume (Controller No.7) and Expression (Controller No.11) are essentially the same thing. However, when exporting your work as a MIDI file for use on another computer, keyboard or sound module, it is best to use Volume as a master function, to control the overall picture, and Expression for the dynamic changes within that picture. This allows the end user to adjust the balance of individual instruments on their equipment – what sounds loud on your gear may sound quiet on theirs – without spoiling the dynamic content of the recorded data.

A foot pedal (much like on a real piano) can be used to control these parameters in real time when playing from a keyboard. Being the imperfect keyboard player that I am, I prefer to add these changes afterwards by either using the MIDI mixer, the Key Editor or Controller Editor.

Project 2 – a rock score

6

Musical objectives
- Sequence a rock score comprised of piano, guitar, bass guitar and drums.
- Achieve a realistic interpretation of a live rock band.

New Cubase skills
- Use the LM-9 Drum Kit.
- Load the General MIDI Drum Map.
- View Parts and enter beats in the Drum Editor.
- View Mapped Drums in the Score Editor.
- Set Volume, Pan and Velocity settings in the Track Inspector.
- Use Transposition in the Track Inspector.

Preparation
- From the CD, copy the folder named 'project2' to your computer.
- On your computer, create a folder called 'mywork2' or something similar in which to save your work.
- Prepare an Arrange window containing four MIDI Tracks and corresponding Channels.
- On the Transport Bar, set the Time Signature to 4/4.
- Our tempo for this piece is 100bpm. Set this in the Mastertrack [Edit>List Mastertrack]. Scroll the tempo to 100. The Timesign will show 4/4 if it has already been set on the Transport Bar. Close the Mastertrack Editor and scroll the Tempo on the Transport Bar to a suitable number. I have chosen 90 bpm. You may prefer something slower.
- Go to the Quantize dialogue box. [Edit>Preferences>MIDI>Quantize] and select the Default setting.
- In the 'mywork2' folder save as Song File – myproj2.all – or something similar.

If your music reading skills are not too hot don't be put off by the score (Figures 6.1 and 6.2). Load project2/project2.all – the finished thing – and have a listen.

You will need to set the Output column to the VST Instrument called Universal Sound Module for Tracks 1 to 4, and the Drum Tracks using Channel 10 to the LM-9 otherwise you may not hear anything!

It's Closing Time

Figure 6.1 Project 2 – Score; page 1

Page 2

Figure 6.2 Project 2 – Score; page 2

Play it through several times and practise reading the score (Figures 6.1 and 6.2) at the same time. When you are more familiar with the tune, work through the project. If you get stuck, save your work and return to the finished version for reference.

Take 1

• Select Track 2 (Ch 2) and rename it 'Left Hand'.

Track Inspector
Output: USM
Program: 1
Patchname: Acoustic Grand Piano

Status Bar
Quantize [8]

Transport Bar
Locators: (L) Left 1.1.1. (R) 5.1.1

Activate the Master Button to listen at the correct tempo

• Record the first four bars of the left hand part (Figure 6.1). It's the same four bars used in Project 1 (page 14, Figures 3.3 and 3.4). If you want, copy and paste them over.
• Activate the Master button on the Transport Bar to listen at the correct tempo. If it's not as tight as you would like apply Quantization repeatedly until you're happy.

• Save song – compare with project2/1.arr.

When loading *my* Cubase Arrange files into *your* Song file version for comparison, remember to:

1 Check that the Universal Sound Module and any other VST Instruments needed have been loaded.
2 Ensure the Output column displays the USM and any other VST Instruments needed.
3 To avoid confusion, close down *my* Arrange file version before any further saving of *your* Song file.

Check that the Universal Sound Module has been loaded ...

... and ensure the Output columns display the USM

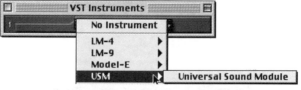

Take 2

- Select Track 1 (Ch 1) and rename it 'Right Hand'.

Track Inspector
Output: USM
Program: 1
Patchname: Acoustic Grand Piano

Status Bar
Quantize [8]

Transport Bar
Locators: (L) Left 1.1.1. (R) 5.1.1

- Deactivate the Master button on the Transport Bar and reset to your preferred tempo. Now record the first four bars of the right hand piano part (Figure 6.1). Again, it's the same four bars used in Project 1 (page 16, Figures 3.6 and 3.8). If you want, copy and paste them over. Listen back and apply Iterative Quantization.

- Save Song – compare with project2/2.arr.

Take 3

- Return to Track 2, set the Locators to 5.1.1 and 9.1.1 and record the next four bars of the left hand part.

Bars 5 – 9 of the left hand piano part

Left Hand

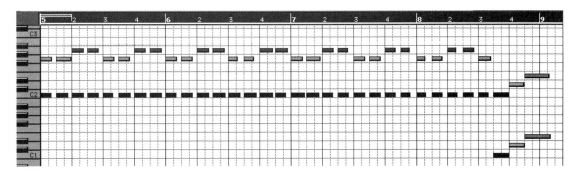

- Switch to Track 1 and record the right hand part between the same Locator set up. If necessary, apply Iterative Quantize to both.

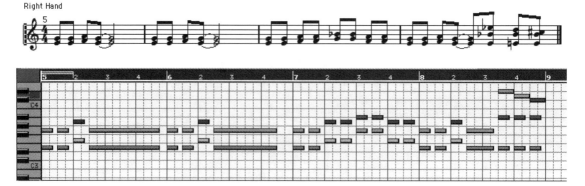

Bars 5 – 9.of the right hand piano part

Save song – compare with project2/3.arr.

Take 4

- Return to Track 2, set the Locators to 9.1.1 and 13.1.1 and record the next four bars of the left hand part.

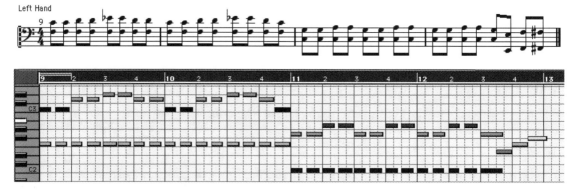

Bars 9 – 13.of the left hand piano part

- Switch to Track 1 and record the right hand part between the same Locator set up. If necessary, apply Iterative Quantize to both.

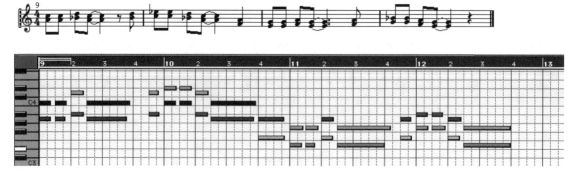

Bars 9 – 13.of the right hand piano part

- Save song – compare with project2/4.arr.

Take 5

- Return to Track 2, set the Locators between 13.1.1 and 17.1.1 and record the next four bars of the left hand part.

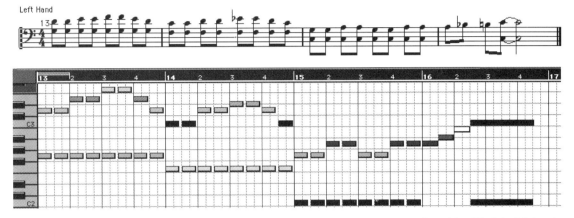

Bars 13 – 17 of the left hand piano part

- Switch to Track 1 and record the right hand part between the same Locator set up. If necessary, apply Iterative Quantize to both.

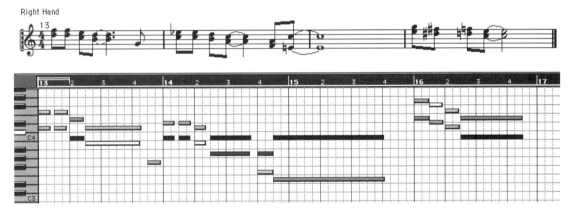

Bars 13 – 17 of the right hand piano part

- Save song – compare with project2/5.arr

Take a look at the Guitar part on the score (Figures 6.1 and 6.2). Apart from bar 8, it's all in two part harmony. No doubt a real guitarist would have played a few more notes but for our purposes it's fine. I chose the General MIDI preset 31 – Distortion Guitar – for extra bite.

Take 6

- Select Track 3 (Ch 3) and rename it 'Guitar'.

Track Inspector
Output: USM
Program: 31
Patchname: Distortion Guitar

Status Bar
Quantize [8]

Transport Bar
Locators: (L) 5.1.1 (R) 9.1.1

- Record the four bars between the Locators.

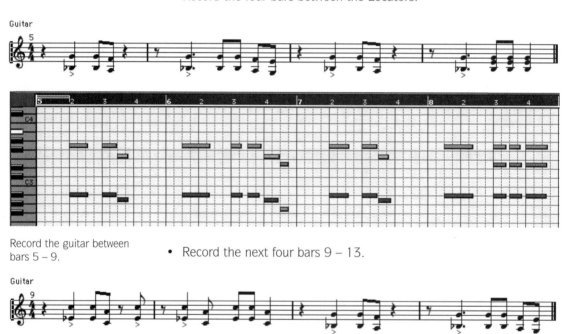

Record the guitar between
bars 5 – 9.

- Record the next four bars 9 – 13.

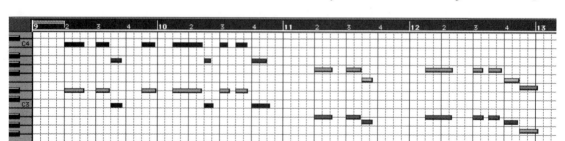

Record the guitar between
bars 9 – 13.

- Record the next four bars 13 – 17.
- Apply Iterative Quantization to all three Parts until you are happy with the result.

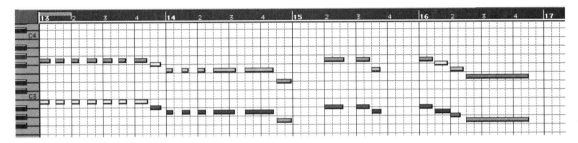

- Save song – compare with project2/6.arr.

Record the guitar between bars 13 – 17.

For the Bass Guitar I chose Electric Bass (pick) from the USM sound set. You may prefer another. A synth bass works just as well with this simple line. You can of course change the Output Port to VB-1, a virtual bass guitar that comes with Cubase (Figure 6.3).

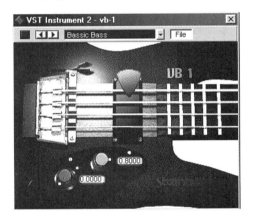

Figure 6.3 Virtual bass instrument – the VB-1

Take 7

- Select Track 4 (Ch 4) and rename it 'Bass Guitar'.

Track Inspector
Output: USM
Program: 35
Patchname: Electric Bass (pick)
Transp –12

INFO

Note the transposition of –12 in the Track Inspector for Take 7. The reason for this? Bass Guitar is notated 1 octave higher than it actually sounds.

Status Bar
Quantize [8]

Transport Bar
Locators: (L) 5.1.1 (R) 9.1.1

- Record the four bars between the Locators.

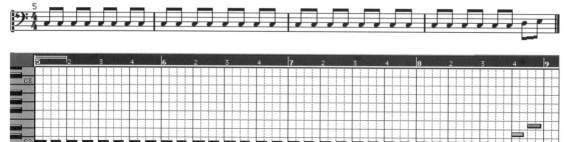

Record the bass between bars
5 – 9.

- Record the next four bars 9 – 13.

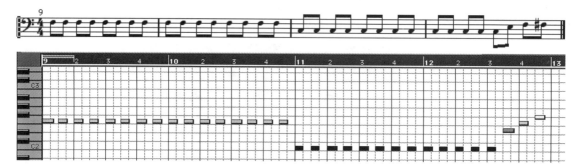

Record the bass between bars
9 – 13 (above) ...

... and again between 13 – 17
(below).

- Record the next four bars 13 – 17.
- Apply Iterative Quantization to all three Parts until you are happy
  with the result.

- Save Song – compare with project2/7.arr.

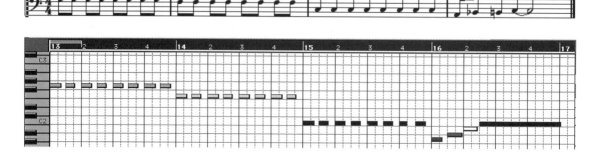

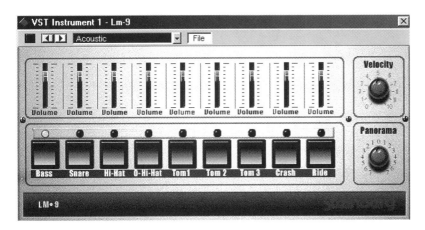

Figure 6.4 A simple drum machine – the LM9.

Adding a new track

Now for the drums. We are out of Tracks so:

• Create a new Track [Structure>Create Track]. A new MIDI Track appears. Instead of using the USM drum kit we will use the LM-9 kit that comes with Cubase VST 5.
• Add the LM-9 to your VST Instruments [Panel>VST Instruments] and choose the 'Acoustic' set from the pop-up menu.

Add the LM-9 to your VST Instruments and choose the Acoustic set.

• Ensure that the General MIDI Drum Map is loaded for viewing the score. [File>Open from Library>General MIDI Drum Map].
• Return to Track 5 and set the Output Port to LM-9.

Take 8

• Select Track 5, change the Channel to 10 and rename the Track 'Kick/Snare'.

Track Inspector
Output: LM-9
Patchname: Acoustic

Status Bar
Quantize [8]

Transport Bar
Locators: (L) 5.1.1 (R) 9.1.1

- Play and record the kick and snare drums together (C1 and D1) between the Locators. Listen back and apply Iterative Quantization until the required degree of tightness is achieved. If you find it difficult to play both drums together play them separately, on different passes.

Kick/Snare

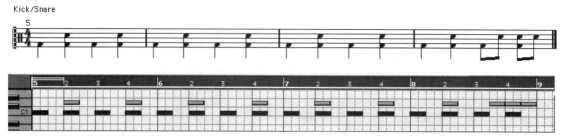

Bars 5 – 9 shown in the Score Edit and Key Edit windows respectively.

Entering notes manually in the Drum Editor

Drum notes can be entered manually in the Drum Editor as an alternative method.

- Select the kick/ksnare Track and create a Part between the Locators [Structure>Create Part].
- Load the General MIDI Drum Map [File>Open from Library>General MIDI Drum Map].

Create a part and load the General MIDI Drum Map.

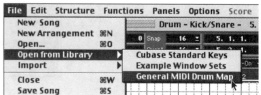

- Open the Drum Editor [Edit>Drum].

 Use the Drum Stick Tool to enter and delete notes.

- Save song.

- The next four bars (9.1.1 – 13.1.1) are the same. You can either record them again or do it the quick way and duplicate the previous Part.
- Play and record the last four bars (13.1.1 – 17.1.1)
- Apply Iterative Quantization until tight.

Bars 5 – 9 shown in the Drum Editor.

Kick/Snare

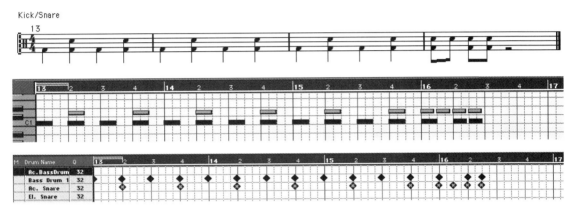

Use the Drum Editor to view a graphical representation of the Parts. Also, have a look at the Score view. With the Score open select [Score>Staff Presets>Drums] to view the Parts as standard drum notation. If you played it correctly, it should look the same as our score. If not, check that you have the GM Drum Map loaded.

Bars 13 – 17 shown in the Score Edit, Key Edit and Drum Edit windows respectively.

- Save song – compare with project2/8.arr.

Take 9

- Create another MIDI Track. Change the Channel to 10 and rename the Track 'Hi-Hat'.

Track Inspector
Output: LM-9
Patchname: Acoustic

Status Bar
Quantize [8]

Transport Bar
Locators: (L) 5.1.1 (R) 9.1.1

- Record the Closed Hi-Hat (F#1) between the Locators. Listen back and apply Iterative Quantization until the required degree of tightness is achieved.

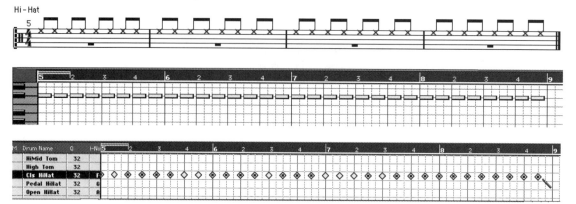

Bars 5 – 9 of HiHat shown in the Score Edit, Key Edit and Drum Edit windows respectively.

- Save song.

- The next four bars (9.1.1 – 13.1.1) are the same. You can either record them again or do it the quick way and duplicate the previous Part.
- The next three bars (13.1.1 – 16.1.1) are also the same. Either record them again or maybe duplicate the previous Part and delete the notes in the last bar (bar 17) in one of the Editors.
- Apply Iterative Quantization until tight.

- Save song – compare with project2/9.arr.

Take 10

Create another MIDI Track. Change the Channel to 10 and rename the Track 'Toms'.

Track Inspector
Output: LM-9
Patchname: Acoustic

Status Bar
Quantize [8]

Transport Bar
Locators: (L) 4.1.1 (R) 5.1.1

Toms

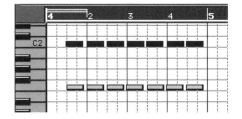

Toms shown in the Score Edit,
Key Edit and Drum Edit
windows respectively.

- Play and record both Toms together (notes C2 and F1). If necessary,
  apply Iterative Quantization.

- Save song – compare with load project2/10.arr.

Take 11

Create another MIDI Track. Change the Channel to 10 and rename the
Track 'Crash Cymbal'.

Track Inspector
Output: LM-9
Patchname: Acoustic

Status Bars
Quantize [8]

Transport Bar
Locators: (L) 5.1.1 (R) 13.1.1

- They're not marked on the score but why not record the odd crash
  cymbal? (C#2) On the first beat of bar 5 maybe. I placed one at the
  beginning of bar 9 and on the fourth 1/8th note of bar 16. If
  necessary, apply Iterative Quantization.

Crash Cymbal Part.

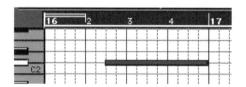

M	Drum Name	Q	I-Note	16		2		3		4		17
	Ride Cymbl1	32	D#2									
	Ride Bell	32	F2									
	Ride Cymbl2	32	B2									
	CrashCymbl1	32	C#2			◆						
	CrashCymbl2	32	A2									
	SplashCymbl	32	G2									
	ChineseCymb	32	E2									

- Save song.

To achieve a balanced result I reduced the velocities of the piano (both Tracks) by –10 in the Track Inspector and their volume to 75 and separated the guitar and piano in the stereo picture by panning them R16 and L16 leaving the bass and drums in the centre. Experiment with your own recording.

- Save song – compare with project2/11.arr.

Project 3 – a jazz funk score

7

Musical objectives
- Achieve a realistic interpretation of a short jazz funk score comprising rhythm section and 'horns' – trumpet, tenor sax and trombone.
- Improvise 1 bar 'breaks' in the horn parts using a blues scale.
- Achieve a satisfactory mix – volume balance and stereo picture.

New Cubase skills
- Use AQ (Automatic Quantize) on the Transport Bar.
- Use Over Quantize and Cubase Pre-set Grooves.
- Use the MIDI Trackmixer.
- Use the Randomize function in the Extended Track Inspector.

Preparation
- From the CD, copy the folder named 'project3' to your computer.
- On your computer, create a folder called 'mywork3' or something similar in which to save your work.
- Prepare an Arrange window containing 6 MIDI Tracks and corresponding Channels plus three MIDI Tracks (reserved for drums) set to Channel 10.
- On the Transport Bar, set the Time Signature to 4//4.
- In the Mastertrack [Edit>List Mastertrack], scroll the tempo to 95 bpm. The Time sign will show 4/4 if it has already been set on the Transport Bar.
- In the 'mywork3' folder, save as Song File – myproj3.all – or something similar.

Let's take a look at the score. (Figures 7.1 – 7.4) It looks complicated – right? Don't be put off. This kind of music always looks horrendous written down. Once you hear it things make more sense.
  Load project3/project3.all and have a good listen.

Figures 7.1 and 7.2 Pages 1 and 2 of the jazz funk score

You will need to set the Output columns to the VST Instrument called Universal Sound Module for Tracks 1 to 6, and the drum Tracks using Channel 10 to the LM-9 otherwise you may not hear anything!

Page 3

Page 4

Play it several times and follow the score. Sounds easier than it looks doesn't it? Mute and solo Tracks to hear individual sections, Tracks and Parts.

The 'Groove' is important here and it may be best to start this project with drums and bass.

Figures 7.3 and 7.4 Pages 3 and 4 of the jazz funk score

Take 1

- Select Track 7 (Ch10) and rename it 'Kick/Snare'.

Track Inspector
Output: LM-9
Patchname: Acoustic

Status Bar
Quantize [8]

Transport Bar
Locators: (L) 1.1.1 (R) 9.1.1
Activate AQ

- Select 'Over Quantize' and record the first eight bars of the kick (C1) and snare (D1) drums (Figures 7.1 and 7.2).

- Save song – compare with project3/1.arr.

When loading *my* Cubase Arrange files into *your* Song file version for comparison, remember to:

1 Check that the Universal Sound Module and any other VST Instruments needed have been loaded.
2 Ensure the Output columns displays the USM or any other VST Instruments needed.
3 To avoid confusion, close down *my* Arrange file version before any further saving of *your* Song file.

Take 2

Select Track 6 (Ch 6) and rename it 'Slap Bass'.

Track Inspector
Output: USM
Program: 38
Patchname: Slap Bass 2
Transp. –12

Status Bar
Quantize [8]

Transport Bar
Locators: (L) 1.1.1 (R) 9.1.1
Activate AQ

- Record the first eight bars of the bass part.

- Save song – compare with project3/2.arr.

That's a basic drum and bass pattern established. Now for the horns. Trumpet first.

Take 3

- Select Track 1 (Ch 1) and rename it 'Trumpet'.

Track Inspector
Output: USM
Program: 57
Patchname: Trumpet

Status Bar
Quantize [16]

Transport Bar
Locators (L) 1.1.1 (R) 4.1.1

- Record the first three bars of trumpet between the Locators (Figure 7.1). Apply Quantization. I have chosen Groove 4) 16th+8 for my Quantizing Type. You may prefer something else. Experiment.

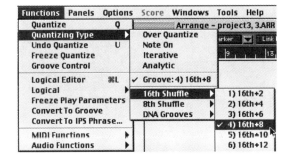

- Copy the Part to bar 5 (5 – 8).

- Save song – compare with project3/3.arr.

A very useful set of pre-defined grooves is supplied with Cubase VST. The figure below shows bar 1 of the unquantized trumpet Part displayed in the List Editor. Compare those positions after Groove 4) 16th+8 has been applied.

Before quantizing ...

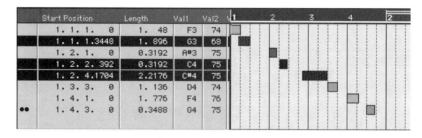

... and after

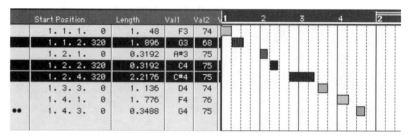

Take 4

• Select Track 2 (Ch 2) and rename it 'Tenor Sax'.

Track Inspector
Output: USM
Program: 67
Patchname: Tenor Sax

Status Bar
Quantize [16]

Transport Bar
Locators (L) 1.1.1 (R) 4.1.1

You may have noticed the figure 8 just below the treble clef sign at the beginning of the tenor sax staff. This tells us that the tenor sax is notated one octave higher on the score than it actually sounds. There are two choices here.

1 Play the part 1 octave lower on your keyboard.
2 Enter a value of –12 in the Track Inspector before you play the part.

- Record the first three bars of tenor sax (Figure 7.1). Apply Quantization – Groove 4) 16th+8.
- Copy the Part to bar 5 (5 – 8).

- Save song – compare with project3/4.arr.

Take 5

- Select Track 3 (Ch 3) and rename it 'Trombone'.

Track Inspector
Output: USM
Program: 58
Patchname: Trombone

Status Bar
Quantize [16]

Transport Bar
Locators (L) 1.1.1 (R) 4.1.1

- Record the first four bars of trombone (Figure 7.1). Apply Quantization – Groove 4) 16th+8.
- Copy the Part to bar 5 (5 – 8).

'Hang on a minute,' I hear you say, 'what about the notes in bar 4? We've missed them out!' True, but that's a 'solo break' and we'll record it separately. All in good time!

- Save song – compare with project3/5.arr.

Take 6

- Set the Locators at (L) 9.1.1 (R) 13.1.1 and record the kick/snare and bass parts (Figure 7.3). Use the same Quantization setting as Take 1.

- Save song – compare with project3/6.arr.

Take 7

- Set Locators to (L) 9.1.1 (R) 13.1.1 and record the trumpet, tenor sax and trombone (Figure 7.3) on their respective Tracks and as before, apply Quantization – Groove 4) 16th+8.

- Save song – compare with project3/7.arr.

Take 8

- Set Locators to (L) 14.1.1 (R) 17.1.1 and record the last three bars of kick/snare and bass parts (Figure 7.4). Use 'Over Quantize' [8].
- Save song.
- Record the last three bars of trumpet, tenor sax and trombone (Figure 7.4). Quantization set to Groove 4) 16th+8 again.

- Save song – compare with project3/8.arr.

Take 9

- Select Track 4 (Ch 4) and rename it 'Guitar'.

Track Inspector
Output: USM
Program: 31
Patchname: Distortion Guitar

Status Bar
Quantize [16]

Transport Bar
Locators (L) 1.1.1 (R) 4.1.1

Guitar parts are usually written an octave higher than they sound, even on a concert score. In this case, as we are playing a keyboard, it has been left at concert pitch. Play exactly as written.

- Record the first three bars of guitar (Figure 7.1) and apply Groove 4) 16th+8 Quantization. If you have problems playing against the brass parts, mute them. Copy the recorded Part to bars 5 (5 – 8) and 14 (14 – 17).
- Go back and set the Locators to (L) 9.1.1 (R) 13.1.1 and record the middle section (Figure 7.3). Apply Quantization Groove 4) 16th +8.

- Save song – compare with project 5/9.arr.

Take 10

- Select Track 5 (Ch 5) and rename it 'Organ'.

Track Inspector
Output: USM
Program: 19
Patchname: Rock Organ

Status Bar
Quantize [8]

Transport Bar
Locators: (L) 1.1.1 (R) 4.1.1
Activate AQ

- Record the organ part using AQ (Figure 7.1). Play it quietly, it's only a supporting part. Reducing the Velocity value in the Track Inspector will help achieve this. Copy the Part to bars 5 (5 – 8) and 14 (14 – 17).
- Set the Locators at (L) 9.1.1 (R) 13.1.1 and record the middle section (see Figure 7.3).

- Save song – compare with project3/10.arr.

Take 11

OK, let's add those 'solo breaks'. You can copy the score or invent your own. You may have noticed that most of the Parts are made up from the 'blues scale' beginning on G (G Bb C C# D F G). Try using it for your improvised breaks.

- Select the trombone Track (Ch 3) and set the Locators at (L) 4.1.1 (R) 5.1.1 and record a simple improvised break (Figure 7.1). Leave it unquantized for a realistic effect.
- Do the same between (L) 8.1.1 (R) 9.1.1 – Tenor Sax – and (L) 13.1.1 (R) 14.1.1 – Trumpet (Figures 7.2 and 7.4).

- Save song – compare with project3/11.arr.

Take 12

- Select Track 8 (Ch 10) and rename it 'Hi-Hat'.

Track Inspector
Output: LM-9
Patchname: Acoustic

Status Bar
Quantize: [16]

Transport Bar
Locators: (L) 1.1.1 (R) 4.1.1

- Record the Hi-Hat part (Figure 7.1) – open (A#1) closed (F#1) – and apply Groove 4) 16th+8 and copy the Part to bar 5 (5 – 8) and 14 (14 – 17).

TIP:

If you find it difficult to play with a light touch, reducing the Velocity value in the Track Inspector before you play will affect your performance in real time. Experiment with different values.

TIP

Try adding some pitch bend from your MIDI keyboard as you play the breaks. A trombonist will typically use his 'slide' for glissando (Glissando – a posh word for 'slide'.) effects in solos. View the Pitch Bend data in the List, Key or Controller Editors.

- Set the Locators at (L) 9.1.1 (R) 13.1.1 and record the middle section (Figure 7.1). Apply Groove 4)16th+8.

- Save song – compare with project3/12.arr.

Last but not least add the crash cymbal.

Take 13

- Select Track 9 and rename it 'Crash Cymbal'

Track Inspector
Output: LM-9
Patchname: Acoustic

Status Bar
Quantize [8]

Transport Bar
Locators: (L) 9.1.1 (R) 13.1.1
Activate AQ

- Select 'Over Quantize' and record the cymbal crashes (A2) (Figure 7.3).

- Save song – compare with project3/13.arr.

The mix

On Project 2 we set up a volume and pan mix using the Track Inspector. However, there is another more intuitive way:

TIP

When mixing, keep the lead instrument loudest. In this case, the trumpet.

- Open the MIDI Track Mixer [Panels>MIDI Track Mixer]. A virtual mixing desk appears with a fader for each Channel used in the Arrange page. To achieve a nice balance I set my fader levels as follows: trumpet 120, tenor sax 115, trombone 115, guitar 40, organ 46, slap bass 101, drums 105.

Of course, your levels will depend on how you played the parts into Cubase. Experiment until you achieve a balance.

My stereo picture for this piece is straightforward: drums and bass in the centre, guitar L32, organ R31, trumpet in the centre, tenor sax L14 and trombone R13.

Figure 7.5 Fader positions for the jazz funk score

A finishing touch. The brass section is sounding really tight. Too tight maybe. Let's humanize it!

- Open the Extended Inspector (Figure 7.6). Click on the button just beneath the word 'Snap' in the Status Bar.
- Select Track 1 – Trumpet 1. Go to the Randomize section and leaving it 'off' for the moment, set –3 (min) and 3 (max). Select 'Position' and it will change to –120 and 120. This represents the number of 'ticks' we are allowing either side of the quantized notes to be randomised.
- Do the same for the tenor sax and trombone Tracks. I chose to apply the same value to the bass Track, just to loosen things up. Experiment (be careful – go too far and the bass player sounds like he's had one beer too many!)

- Save song – compare with project3/mix.arr.

Figure 7.6

Project 4 – a classical score

8

Musical objectives
- Sequence a short extract from Mozart's Clarinet Concerto.
- Achieve a convincing interpretation of a string orchestra and solo clarinet.
- Position the instruments in a realistic stereo picture.

New Cubase skills
- Use Transposition in the Track Inspector.
- Apply Compression in the Track Inspector.
- Apply Legato to slurred notes using either the Key or Score Editors.
- Automate the MIDI Track Mixer and create a Track Mix.

Preparation
- From the CD, copy the folder named 'project4' to your computer.
- On your computer create a folder called 'mywork4' or something similar in which to save your work.
- Prepare an Arrange window containing six MIDI Tracks and corresponding Channels.
- On the Transport Bar, set the Time Signature to 3/4.
- Our tempo for this piece is 65bpm. Set this in the Mastertrack [Edit>List Mastertrack]. This style of music needs to be played accurately and at this tempo, I recommend activating AQ (Automatic Quantize) on the Transport Bar. We can loosen it up later if need be. The Timesign will show 3/4 if it has already been set on the Transport Bar. If not, change it. Close the Mastertrack Editor and scroll the tempo on the Transport Bar to a suitable number.
- In the 'mywork4' folder, save as Song File – myproj4.all or something similar.

OK this is Mozart. Don't be scared. It's not difficult. It's slow for a start!
  To begin with, load project4/project4.all and have a listen as you view the score. Play it through several times until it becomes familiar.

Page 1

Clarinet Concerto

Mozart

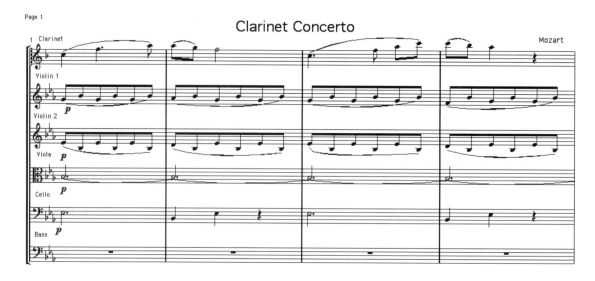

Page 2

Figure 8.1 and 8.2 Pages 1 and 2 of the Mozart concerto

You will need to set the Output column to the VST Instrument called Universal Sound Module for all the Tracks otherwise you may not hear anything!

Figures 8.3 and 8.4 Pages 3 and 4 of the Mozart concerto

The clarinet solo is in from bar 1, so let's get that down and take it from there.

Take 1

- Select Track (Ch 1) and rename it 'Clarinet'.

Track Inspector
Output: USM
Program: 72
Patchname: Clarinet
Transp. –2
Compr. 75%

Take a look at the score (Figures 8.1 – 8.4). The strings are written in Eb (three flats) and the clarinet in F (one flat). This is because clarinets are pitched in Bb. When Bb is played on the piano a clarinet plays the note C. Wiithout getting into the complexities of a thorough explanation, what this means is we read and play the score as written and transpose it down a tone. To achieve this it is necessary to enter –2 in the Track Inspector. In order to achieve a nice smooth classical clarinet sound we also need to apply 75% compression.

Apply compression to the clarinet Part

- Record the first four bars of the clarinet part (Figure 8.1). Play in a nice legato style. Any overlapping notes can be cleaned up afterwards.
- Set the Locators to cycle between 5.1.1 and 9.1.1 and record the next four bars (Figure 8.2). Join the two resulting parts together with the Glue Tool to make a Part eight bars long.

Listen back. I mentioned earlier about woodwind players articulating with their tongues. Where a slur joins a group of notes only the first note is slurred. Some editing is necessary to achieve this effect.

- Using either the Score or Key Editors, select all the notes under each slur, except the last, and apply Legato [Functions>MIDI Functions>Note Length>Legato].

- The following eight bars are an exact repetition of the first so copy the new part (bars 1 – 9) [Structure>Repeat Parts] to bar 9. We now have 16 bars. Clean up any overlapping notes (impossible on a clarinet!) by viewing the Parts in the Key Editor and applying Functions>MIDI Functions>Note Length>Del. Overlaps (mono) and Del. Overlaps (poly).

- Save song – compare with project4/1.arr.

> ## TIP
>
> *A*lways leave the last note under a slur unselected before applying Legato. Think about it!

When loading *my* Cubase Arrange files into *your* Song file version for comparison, remember to:

1 Check that the Universal Sound Module and any other VST Instruments needed have been loaded.
2 Ensure the Output columns display the USM and any other VST Instruments needed.
3 To avoid confusion, close down *my* Arrange file version before any further saving of *your* Song file.

Take 2

- Select Track (Ch 2) and rename it 'violin 1'.

Track Inspector
Output: USM
Program: 49
Patchname: String Ensemble 1
Compr. 75%

Status Bar
Quantize [8]

Transport Bar
Locators: (L) Left 1.1.1. (R) 9.1.1
Activate AQ

We are simulating a small string orchestra here so we use Program 49 – String Ensemble – and not an individual instrument. You can of course use single instruments if you wish, but the effect will be somewhat thinner. The nature of this concerto, I think, benefits from a rather more lush background.

- Record the first eight bars of the violin 2 part (Figures 8.1 and 8.2). Break it down into smaller sections if necessary. Again I have applied 75% compression in the Track Inspector for smoothness.
- Listen back, and as with the clarinet part, apply legato to the slurred notes and clean up with the Del. Overlaps (mono) and Del. Overlaps (poly) functions.

- Save song – compare with project4/2.arr.

Take 3

- Select Track (Ch 3) and rename it 'violin 2'

Track Inspector
Output: USM
Program: 49
Patchname: String Ensemble 1
Compr. 75%

Status Bar
Quantize [8]

Transport Bar
Locators: (L) Left 1.1.1. (R) 9.1.1
Activate AQ

- Record the first eight bars of the violin 1 part (Figures 8.1 and 8.2). Apply Legato and clean up as in Take 2.
- Save song – compare with project4/take3.arr.

Take 4

- Select Track (Ch 4) and rename it 'viola'.

TIP

A n easy way to read and play from the alto clef. In the Track Inspector, enter –10 in the Transpose box and play the part as if reading the treble clef.

Track Inspector
Output: USM
Program: 49
Patchname: String Ensemble 1
Compr. 75%

Status Bar
Quantize [8]

Transport Bar
Locators: (L) Left 1.1.1. (R) 9.1.1
Activate AQ

Alto clef sign

- Record the first eight bars of the viola part (Figures 8.1 and 8.2). Viola parts are written in the alto clef. Middle C is on the middle line of the staff.

As with the violins, apply Legato and clean up where necessary.

- Save song – compare with project4/4.arr.

Take 5

- Select Track (Ch 5) and rename it 'Cello'.

Track Inspector
Output: USM
Program: 49
Patchname: String Ensemble 1
Compr. 75%

Status Bar
Quantize [8]

Transport Bar
Locators: (L) Left 1.1.1. (R) 9.1.1
Activate AQ

- Record the first eight bars of the cello part (Figures 8.1 and 8.2). If you have played it carefully, legato need not be applied. However you may have to use the Del. Overlaps (mono) and Del. Overlaps (poly) functions. I did!

- Save song – compare with project4/5.arr.

Take 6

- Select Track 2 (Ch 2) 'Violin 1'.

Track Inspector
Output: USM
Program: 49
Patchname: String Ensemble 1
Compr. 75%

Status Bar
Quantize [16]

Transport Bar
Locators: (L) Left 9.1.1. (R) 17.1.1
Activate AQ

- Record the remaining eight bars of violin 1 (Figures 8.3 and 8.4). (Note: Quantize Value is now 16) Break it down into four bar sections and use the Glue Tool if you wish. Apply Legato and clean up note lengths.

- Save song

Take a look at the score again. Bars 9 – 16 of violin 2 are the same as bars 1 – 8 of violin 1. No point in making extra work!

- Select the violin 1 (bars 1 – 9) Part and drag a copy over to bar 9 on Track 3 (violin 2).
- There are of course five notes to add to this new Part in bar 16. Set the Locators between 16 and 17 and overdub them. Apply Legato and clean up any over lapped notes.
- To avoid confusion, it's a good idea to re-name the Part 'Violin 2' and change the colour accordingly.

Choosing colours

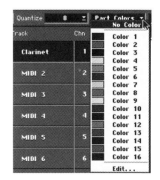

It's often a good idea to organize Tracks and Parts by colour. Select a Track or Part and click on the Part Colors box and choose from the drop-down menu.

Another glance at the score also tells us that the viola Part between bars 9 and 16 is also a duplication of the violin 2 Part between bars 1 and 8.

- Select the violin 2 (bars 1 – 9) Part and drag a copy over to bar 9 on Track 4 (viola).
- This time there are five notes to delete in bar 16. Selecting them in

either the Key or Score Editor and pressing the delete key on your computer keyboard is probably the easiest method of doing this. You may well need to lengthen the remaining note in this bar. Selecting it in the Key Editor and resizing with the Pencil Tool is probably the simplest way of doing this.

- Again, it's a good idea to re-name the Part 'Viola' and change the colour accordingly.

- Save song – compare with project4/6.arr.

Take 7

- Select Track 5 (Ch 5) 'Cello'.

Track Inspector
Output: USM
Program: 49
Patchname: String Ensemble 1
Compr. 75%

Status Bar
Quantize [8]

Transport Bar
Locators: (L) Left 9.1.1. (R) 17.1.1
Activate AQ

- Record bars 9 – 17 of the cello part (Figures 8.3 and 8.4). Clean up.
- Save song – compare with project4/7.arr.

Take 8

- Select Track 6 (Ch 6) and rename 'Double Bass'.

Track Inspector
Output: USM
Program: 49
Patchname: String Ensemble 1
Transp. -12
Compr. 75%

Status Bar
Quantize [8]

Transport Bar
Locators: (L) Left 9.1.1. (R) 17.1.1
Activate AQ

Have a look at the double bass Part on the score. You have probably noticed that it looks identical to the cello part above it. Well it is, but with one exception. The double bass sounds an octave lower than it is written. We now have a choice. We either record the bass part in the usual way or copy the cello Part to Track 7 and transpose it down one octave.

Although it takes a little longer, I prefer the first option. Why? Because the velocities and note lengths will be different and this adds to the overall realism of the sequence. Two parts with identical data, playing together, often sound naff!

- Record the double bass part between bars 9 – 17 (Figures 8.3 and 8.4). Ensure that Transposition is set to –12 in the Track Inspector. Clean up any overlaps.

- Save song – compare with project4/8.arr.

The mix

Open the MIDI Track Mixer [Panels>MIDI Track Mixer]. Six Channels and corresponding faders appear.

Now this is a clarinet solo, so obviously that instrument needs to be louder than the others. The first eight measures of the strings are marked *piano* (quiet). We will now create a simple automated Track Mix.

Important! On the Transport Bar set the Song Pointer to 1.1.1.

I set the faders to following levels: clarinet – 115, violin1 – 95, violin 2 – 95, viola – 95, cello – 95, bass – 95. You may well need to set your faders to different levels for a nice balance, depending on the velocity recorded when you played the parts into Cubase. Whatever you decide, keep the clarinet prominent.

Set transposition to –12

TIP

When mixing, keep the solo instrument – in this case the clarinet – in the centre of the stereo picture and, if necessary, raise its volume for prominence.

Setting the faders for a good balance

In a real string orchestra 1st and 2nd violins are positioned to the left of the conductor and the viola and cellos to the right. The double basses are behind the violas and cellos.

Adjust the pan control – use the oblong box above the faders

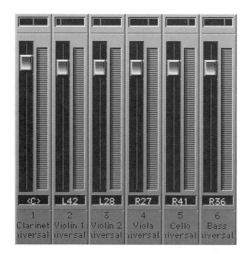

- To achieve something similar in our stereo picture adjust the pan control – use the oblong box above the faders – to the following: clarinet <C> in the centre. It's his/her big moment! Violin 1 – L42, violin 2 – L28, viola – R27, cello – R41, double bass – R36.
- Press the button marked 'Write'.
- Turn it off. In the Arrange page. You will now see an extra Track entitled ' Track Mix'.

Refer to the score. In bar 8 (at 8.1.3. to be precise) the strings change to *forte* (loud).

- Position the Song Pointer at 8.1.3.
- Raise the fader levels for the strings; in my example they are changed to: violin1 – 105, violin 2 – 105, viola – 105, cello – 105, bass – 105.
- Press the button marked 'Write'.

- Turn it off.
- Turn the button named 'Read' on.
- Play the piece from the beginning and sit back and gaze in wonderment as the faders move all by themselves. I love it! Could watch them all day. Sad really isn't it?

- Save song – compare with project4/mix.arr.

TIP

To ensure the MIDI Mixer faders always work when you load up a song or arrangement make sure that the 'Read' button is activated.

Ideas – how to get them

9

So far we have talked about and sequenced other people's music – well mine actually, apart from the classical stuff – and I'm sure you are itching to put some of the topics covered into practice by composing music of your own. Before you can start doing this you will need ideas. No doubt some of you will have dozens of ideas already. Many people though, find it difficult to be inventive and will either stare blankly at the screen or doodle for hours with nothing to show for it at the end. 'I can't think of anything,' they say.

The old saying, 'Composing is 1% inspiration and 99% hard work' is spot on. Beethoven for example – a creative genius if ever there was one – would tortuously re-work a fragment of melody over and over until he considered it perfect. From that one tiny idea a symphony would develop. 1% eureka, 99% hard graft. So it is for the rest of us in most cases.

So how do we get ideas for compositions in the first place? Can we use Cubase? Will Cubase give us ideas? Well it might. It's not my favourite way to start but it undoubtedly works for some. If you are constructing loop based techno or dance music then using sample CDs with pre-recorded material is the obvious way to go. However, this will not work very well if you've been given a specific brief for a commercial project and you are being paid for it. Other people's licks are not guaranteed to fit the bill. Even if the style of music requires loops and grooves it may well be quicker to invent and record your own. The result is going to be far more original for a start.

At the computer?

A tentative yes. Keep control. A computer running Cubase is a very powerful tool – but a tool is all that it is. It will not, as some mistakenly believe, compose or arrange your music for you. Does a carpenter tell his tools to build him a beautiful piece of furniture, sit back, open a six pack and watch? He'd have a long wait.

One very useful tool within Cubase itself is the Interactive Phrase Synthesizer. It will help generate arpeggios and accompaniments for you, but there is a snag. You've got to feed it the idea in the first place! Oh damn! It's worth trying though. Read the pdf document that comes with Cubase called *Getting Into Details* and experiment with the examples in the IPS folder.

There are special random generator programs available which will turn small ideas into complete compositions of a sort. These are great for experimental music, but I'm sure even the authors of such software would be the first to admit that they are not intended for producing commercial music.

You could import MIDI files into Cubase, chop up the material and re-use it for your own compositions. Not really a good idea though. You could end up in court for breach of copyright!

What about importing classical music MIDI files, chopping those up and re-working them? After all the composers are mostly long dead and the tunes are out of copyright. Well you can I suppose – I can think of one well known composer who does just that, or something similar – but it will not help much if you've been asked to supply a heavy metal background to a motor racing video clip!

No, I'm sorry. Ideas are what we need and where is the best place to get them? ...

Away from the computer?

Leonard Bernstein got them lying on the sofa and staring at the ceiling. When his wife entered the room and asked him what he was doing, he would reply, 'I'm working!'

One thing's for sure. Ideas come more readily if you tell your subconscious that you want them. You may think this is barmy but it works. Give your subconscious instructions. Be specific and set a deadline. Start small. Don't ask for a symphony. You will not get it! Something like:
'I want the beginnings of a tune for a children's song by tomorrow morning'.
The more you develop this habit of asking for ideas the more they begin to come. It's habit forming and self generating. Ideas generate more ideas.

I get ideas first thing in the morning as soon as I wake up. They are usually melodic – I don't dream chord sequences. Fortunately my bedroom is right next door to my studio, so I can leap (or crawl, more like) out of bed, boot up Cubase and record them before breakfast. After the all important pot of tea, I can evaluate these gems, delete them (often the case) or file them away in an 'ideas' folder for later development.

Ideas tend to come in a flash and often fade away just as quick. It's important to act quickly and retain them somehow. If you have a great memory, then fine. If not and you are familiar with music notation then it's a simple matter of keeping a manuscript note pad handy. A portable cassette or mini disk recorder and vocal chords are an alternative.

Don't doodle!

'What a load of cobblers! ' I hear you say. 'I get my ideas at the keyboard. I boot up Cubase, press Record and improvise until the ideas start to flow.' Surely that's the best way to get ideas.

Well good on you. That's great. I envy you. Trouble is, I can't do that, and nor can many others.

For those of you who are good keyboard payers I have only one word of warning. Beware of doodling. Improvising is not composition. Well it is, in a group environment when we tear off a solo on our chosen instrument over a pre-determined chord sequence. For this we generally need a good technique. There lies the problem.

A common scenario. A keyboard player with a fantastic technique sits down at his keyboard to compose and record in Cubase. What happens? Before he knows it his fingers have taken over. They are following patterns that have been learned and subconsciously stored over the years. Out they all come and into Cubase they all go. A half hour later he plays it all back. Has he got a composition at the end of it? I doubt it. Music composed or arranged for a specific purpose generally needs discipline and a degree of planning. A balanced composition, particularly a lengthy one, is rarely conceived as an improvisation. That half hour may have been better spent lying on his back like Leonard Bernstein.

10

Ideas – how to develop them

Dave's got a great idea for a tune. It came like a bolt of lightning while he was waiting for the bus. He hums all the way home – in case he forgets it – and quickly records the melody into Cubase as an eight bar Lead Synth part. 'It's brilliant', he thinks. 'Absoloutely brilliant!' He cycles it round a few times and hits upon a killer bass line. 'Fantastic!', he yells.' He improvises some drums over that and records a funky chord sequence using a favourite guitar patch. 'This is it. This is gonna make me a fortune', he cries. 'Strings! It needs strings,' he bellows, and he sets about adding a string pad. Already his musical canvas is pretty full. He can't think of anything else to add at the moment so he saves the file and goes off to make a cuppa.

A while later Dave returns to his masterpiece. He plays the eight bars. 'Hmm, it's only eight measures long. It definitely needs more, but I can't think of anything else. I know, I'll do a rough mix instead. Something will come to me later.'

Dave sets about the mix and experiments with the levels in the MIDI Trackmixer. He used a VST Instrument for the Synth Lead so he opens up his VST Send Effects rack and adds some Chorus and Reverb effects. A couple of hours later he sits back to have a listen. 'Mmm.. it doesn't sound quite as good now. It's not quite what I had in mind when I was on the bus. Perhaps that bass line needs to be a bit different. ' And so he changes the bass line, which in turn requires a modification to the chord sequence. 'That's better, but hold on.. the melody needs altering to fit that new chord.' Dave alters the melody. Oh dear! Wasn't that the brilliant bit, conceived at the bus stop – 'I'm not sure about that kick drum... it doesn't sound fat enough to me. Where's that article I read in *Sound on Sound* about compression.. it's here somewhere.. Oh well, maybe some EQ instead.'

He's lost the plot now, although I'm not so sure he had one in the first place. It all started so promising as well. What did he do wrong? Well he didn't know where he was going for a start.

Visions – know where you are heading

Those sudden flashes of inspiration, so often likened to thunderbolts, the eureka if you like, are wonderful. Trouble is, once recorded they often turn into short, rather stubborn, fragments of material that refuse to move on. Why? Probably because we have not decided what we want to do in the first place.

The mind works all the time in the background. It will throw up all kinds of great, but totally unrelated ideas. If we decide what we want to write first, and then instruct our subconscious mind to get on with it, we stand a much better chance.

If someone has been commissioned to compose or arrange a piece of music for a specific purpose it is much easier to get going. The plan has been provided, and if you expect to be paid, then you had better stick pretty close to it. If however you want to write for the sheer pleasure of it of it, maybe for practice, then it's a good idea to invent a brief of your own. Give yourself a purpose for writing. Here's a rough guide on how to set about it.

1   Decide exactly what it is you want to write and why. If you are not sure, invent something like 'a local sports shop needs a short radio jingle'. Have a specific shop in mind. You never know, if it turns out well they may decide to invest in a radio advertisement on the strength of your idea.
2   Decide what style the music should take and what instruments or sounds you intend to use. Obviously things may change, but it helps to have a clear mental picture from the outset as to how things will sound.
3   Decide on a basic form. If you can't envisage one mentally, invent one on paper. Keep it simple. ABA maybe. At least that way you have a structure to hang things on.

Now you know where you are heading. You have defined a set of problems to solve with your own skill and musical craftsmanship. Even if the result doesn't quite make it, you can get started and modify it later. As I said earlier, the mind is working constantly, all the time, in the background.   If Dave had followed this route after that initial eureka he would maybe have recorded the broad outline of his project, and having done so had a further brilliant idea to help fill in the details,   perhaps whilst waiting for the bus the next day. That's another thing the mind tends to do – throw up ideas at certain times and places.

Keep moving – work creates work

It is most important to keep moving. It can be a very daunting experience to stare at a blank Arrange page in Cubase and not be able to start. Once you have set your criteria, record anything that it suggests. If you can only think up a tiny fragment of a tune, don't worry. Record it. That's enough. Remember how Beethoven built huge musical masterpieces from just such fragments. Don't dwell on it, but move on. Does that first phrase suggest something else? Does it beg an answer? Can it be repeated? Upside down or back to front. Keep moving. The more you write, even if it is not very good, the easier it will become. Work creates work and ideas produce yet more ideas. You can refine and improve them later.

Repetition and variation

OK so how do we keep things flowing if we can't think of anything? One method of course is simple repetition. It's an essential ingredient of most music. So many beginners are scared stiff to repeat an idea, afraid that it will be boring to do so. On the contrary, an opening phrase will often set an air of expectancy. When this phrase is repeated, the listener's subconscious picks up on it and a basic psychological and emotional sense of musical fulfillment is achieved. Of course it would be utterly boring if the same phrase were repeated endlessly. This is why we also need variation. Repetition and variation, hand in hand. Together they make a very powerful composition tool for almost any style of music.

Keep it simple – details later

As well as moving on it is important to keep it simple. Save the detail until later. If it's melodic material the details such as choice of harmony and rhythm will suggest themselves at a later stage. This is exactly what Dave did not do. He started right. He recorded eight measures of terrific melody, but then stopped and concentrated on the detail instead of moving forward. Paralysis by analysis! In the end he actually ruined the tune he started out with.

Review your work – less is more

Once your idea has been developed and recorded in Cubase, take time to review it objectively. It's usually best left until the next day or even later. You will see a clearer, fresher picture. Those first ideas, great at the time, may require more work. First ideas are not always the best ideas and you may see ways of improving them. Maybe an introduction will suggest itself out of the general thematic material. Intros are paradoxically best left until the end. When composed first they often end up having nothing to do with what follows. Either that or they remain just great intros that go no further.

One more thing. When reviewing your work look for ways of cutting down on unnecessary details. They can usually be found and a bit of ruthless pruning often yields a leaner but more effective composition. If you can't find any, all well and good, but do ask yourself a few questions like: Am I keeping that clever break because it really works? Or am I keeping it because I can't bear to let it go? Be objective. If a particular ingredient is not serving a definite purpose, get rid of it!

Oh! and for goodness sake don't do what Dave did and start mixing after only eight bars. It happens, I can assure you.

Project 5 – a computer game track

11

We will now follow the creative composition process through using a set brief and applying principles and techniques discussed in previous chapters.

The music composed here does not use melodic development to carry it forward, but an additive technique whereby small fragments and cells of material are repeated and transposed to form blocks of material. These blocks are repeated in a loop like fashion and new layers of material are introduced in subsequent cycles to maintain interest. The overall effect is a static one, but that is precisely what we want – atmospheric background music.

Musical objectives
- To build a complete composition with Cubase VST from small fragments and motifs using simple techniques of repetition and harmonic variation.
- Paint an atmospheric musical landscape suitable for background music to match the demands of the brief.
- Achieve clarity and balance through choice of instruments (timbre) stereo placement and mixing.

New Cubase skills
- Use the Key Editor to alter note lengths and velocity in the pursuit of realism.
- Use the MIDI Function; Transpose.
- Route MIDI Cannels to USM Outputs in order to apply VST Send Effects to MIDI Tracks.
- Edit Send Effects.
- Use VST Channel Mixer to apply Send Effects.
- Use the VST Channel Mixer to apply Reverb and Chorus Send Effects.

Preparation
- From the CD, copy the folder named 'project5' to your computer.
- On your computer, create a folder called 'mywork5' or something similar in which to save your work.
- Prepare an Arrange window containing 16 MIDI Tracks and corresponding Channels.
- On the Transport Bar, set the Time Signature to 4/4.

- Our tempo for this piece is 105 bpm. Set this in the Mastertrack [Edit>List>Mastertrack/Graphical Mastertrack].
- In the 'mywork5' folder, save as Song File – myproj5.all or something similar.

The brief

OK, here's the scenario. A computer game company has commissioned you to compose the music for a scene in their latest historical title set in Elizabethan times. The piece must run for a minimum of three minutes.

It's night-time and we see a lone sailor searching a misty quay side for a hidden treasure map. Moored sailing ships bob gently on the tide.

Apart from the sailor, the scene is mostly static. We need something repetitive to underpin the structure. Let's start by recording a short ostinato. A simple line on the lower strings of an acoustic guitar will do nicely.

To gain an overall picture, at this point you may prefer to listen to the finished thing rather than let things unfold. To do so, load project5/project5.all.

You will need to set the Output column to the VST Instrument called Universal Sound Module for all the Tracks otherwise you may not hear anything!

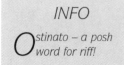

INFO

*O*stinato – a posh word for riff!

Take 1

- Select Track 1 (Ch 1) and rename it 'Guitar 1'.

Track Inspector
Output: USM
Program: 25
Patchname: Acoustic Guitar

Status Bar
Quantize [8]

Transport Bar
Locators:(L) 1.1.1 (R) 5.1.1
Activate AQ

Guitar parts are usually written an octave higher than they sound, even on a concert score. In this case, as we are playing a keyboard, it has been left at concert pitch. Play exactly as written.

- Record the guitar ostinato.

Take 1

Guitar 1

K.G.

Figure 11.1 Record the guitar Part.

Although it's only a one bar repeated figure, it is better to play it four times in succession. This is better than recording it once and duplicating it because the velocities will be more varied and the result will sound more realistic. I have used a tempo of 105 bpm. You may prefer a slower speed for recording.

Depending on your playing style, the result may sound a little stilted if there is too much of a gap between notes. As we know, plucked guitar strings have a resonant quality and are slow to decay.

If this is the case, Select the Part and open the Edit window [Edit> Edit]. If it looks anything like Figure 11.2 – the notes do not quite meet each other – apply Legato [Functions>MIDI>Note Lengths>Legato] to lengthen them. The notes are now placed end to end and should appear like those in Figure 11.3.

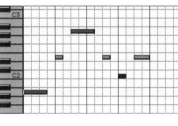

Figure 11.2 Before applying legato …

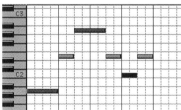

Figure 11.3 … and after.

When loading *my* Cubase Arrange files into *your* Song file version for comparison, remember to:

1 Check that the Universal Sound Module and any other VST Instruments needed have been loaded.
2 Ensure the Output columns display the USM and any other VST Instruments needed.
3 To avoid confusion, close down *my* Arrange file version before any further saving of *your* Song file.

• Save song – compare with project5/1.arr.

OK we've made a start. What next? It's night time, it's misty.... How about some minor chords over that riff? Simple triads (three note chords) will do. 'But a guitar has six strings' I hear you say. True, but this is not a real guitar and six notes will prove too dense for the simple effect needed to create our moody atmosphere. However, if we use open spacing the triads will produce the depth we need.

Take 2

- Select Track 2 (Ch 2) and rename it 'Guitar 2'.

Track Inspector
Output: USM
Program: 25
Patchname: Acoustic Guitar

Status Bar
Quantize [8]

Transport Bar
Locators: (L) 1.1.1 (R) 5.1.1
Activate AQ

- Record the chord sequence in Figure 11.4.

Guitar 2   # Take 2   K.G.

Figure 11.4 Record Take 2.

Listen to the result. If any notes sound too short, check them by viewing in the Edit window. Unlike Guitar 1, the notes need not line up end to end. If any are obviously too short, then lengthen them with the Pencil tool.

Before lengthening ...

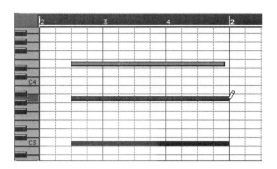

... and after lengthening ...

INFO

How much you can lengthen notes in the Key Editor with the Pencil Tool depends on the Snap value, found on the Functions Bar. In our case a value of 16 is fine.

Snap **16**

- Select both recorded Parts, and use the Repeat command [Structure>Repeat Part(s)] to replicate them. In the 'Repeat selected parts' dialogue box, type 1 for number of copies. Leave 'Ghost Copies' unchecked. A second, identical Part appears on each track between bars 5 and 9.

We now have eight measures of music on Tracks 1 and 2 (Guitar 1 and 2).

- With the Glue Tool, join the two Parts on Track 1 together.

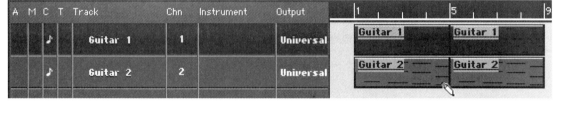

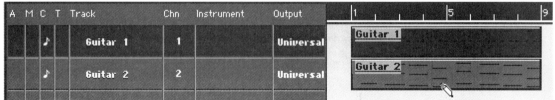

- Repeat the procedure with the two Parts on Track 2.

- Save song – compare with project5/2.arr.

Glueing Parts together – before and after.

OK so far, so good, but we can't repeat the same eight bars indefinitely without some form of variation. On the other hand, we must not overdo it. It's a predominately static scene remember. Let's try repeating the same eight bar sequence but drop the pitch a perfect fourth whilst doing so. That way we keep the minor chords and retain the moody atmosphere.

- Select the Part on Track 1 (bars 1 – 9) and duplicate it [Structure> Repeat Part(s) x1] between bars 9 and 17.
- Select the new Part (9 – 17), and using the Track Inspector, enter a

Figure 11.5 Set a transpose value of −5 in the Track Inspector Transpose box

value of −5 in the Transpose box. There are other ways of doing this, but our chosen method is convenient for now. If we don't like the result, it's easily changed.

• Repeat the above procedure with the Part on Track 2.

Set the Locators to cycle between (L) 1.1.1 (R) 17.1.1 and play the piece back a couple of times. 'Sounds good to me maestro' (as a well known session bass player was fond of saying to the musical director when he wanted to get home early without doing another take!) We're happy with that (well I am anyway) so let's make a commitment! If you were to view the transposed Parts in the Editors at this point they would still show their original pitch, even though we now hear them a perfect fourth below. We'll now make these changes permanent.

• Select the two Parts (bars 9 – 17) on Tracks 1 and 2
• Return the values to zero in the Transpose box in the Track Inspector.
• Open the Transpose dialogue box [Functions>MIDI Functions>Transpose/Velocity] and enter a value of −5 in the Transpose section. Press 'Do' and Exit. Play things back to check the transposition.

Figure 11.6 Enter a value of −5 in the Transpose section of the Transpose/Velocity dialogue box

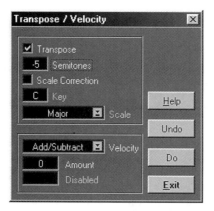

• Save song – compare with project5/3.arr.

We now have 16 bars that can be repeated ad. finitum as long as we dream up interesting variations to overlay.

• Join the two Parts on Track 1 together with the Glue Tool.
• Repeat the procedure on Track 2.
• Copy and Paste the Parts on both Tracks, (bars 1-17) to bar 17.

• Save song – compare with project5/4.arr.

We now have 32 bars of guitars. A different texture perhaps? Strings come to mind, and movement. A rhythmic figure maybe.

Take 3

• Select Track 3 (Ch 3) and rename it 'Strings'.

Track Inspector
Output: USM
Program: 49
Patchname: String Ensemble 1

Status Bar
Quantize [8]

Transport Bar
Locators: (L) 17.1.1 (R) 21.1.1
Activate AQ

• Record Take 3 (Figure 11.7).

Figure 11.7 Record Take 3.

Note the accent on the first eighth note in each measure. Play this with slightly more emphasis than the other notes. Visualize the string section bowing this figure and transfer that to your own playing. Imagine yourself actually playing in that string section. It may sound crazy, but that's how it's done! Cubase will receive these accented notes at slightly higher velocity values.

• Check these velocity values in the Key Editor. If you underplayed the accented notes increase their velocities by selecting the note on the grid and increasing the 'Velo On' value in the Info bar.

We now have another short ostinato figure ready for repetition and variation.

• Save song – compare with – project5/5.arr.

• Copy and Paste the string Part (bars 17 – 21) to bar 21 and glue the two resulting Parts together.
• Copy and Paste this new Part (bars 17 – 25) to bar 25. Once again we have two string Parts.
• Select the second Part (bars 25 – 33) and as we did with the guitars, transpose it down a perfect fourth (–5) in the Transpose Dialogue Box.

Before we continue:

• Select all the Parts on all the Tracks between bars 17 and 33. Copy and Paste them to bar 33.

We now have 48 bars of music.

• Save song – compare with project5/6.arr.

Let's review things so far. We have set a nice background scene through the use of repetitive ostinato figures and limited harmonic variation. Nothing here to distract the game player whilst he noodles around the murky dockyard looking for treasure maps. Even so, to repeat it again would run the risk of sending him to the land of nod. We need some melody, but nothing too intrusive. A fragment lasting around four measures would be ideal. Choice of instrument? What about clarinet. Nice and dark when played in the lower register.

Take 4

• Select Track 4 (Ch 4) and rename it 'Clarinet'.

Track Inspector
Output: USM
Program: 72
Patchname: Clarinet

Status Bar
Quantize [16]

Transport Bar
Locators: (L) 33.1.1 (R) 37.1.1
Activate AQ

• Record Take 4 (Figure 11.8).

Take 4

Figure 11.8 Record Take 4.

Note we have changed the Quantize value in the Status bar to 16. This is to accommodate the sixteenth notes at the beginning of the melody.

Clarinets are members of the woodwind family and a vibrating wooden reed produces the sound. Clarinet players articulate with their tongue, by striking this reed. Observe the written articulation – legato slurs and staccato notes – when playing the part into Cubase VST.

- Copy and Paste the newly recorded clarinet Part (bars 33 – 37) to bar 37 and glue both Parts together.
- Copy and Paste the resulting Part (bars 33 – 41) to bar 41.
- Transpose the second Part (bars 41 – 48) down a perfect fourth (–5) using the Transpose Dialogue Box.

Incidentally, we have now taken the clarinet below its normal range. No matter. In the real world a bass clarinet would play this part. As the GM sound set does not contain a bass clarinet, transposing the normal clarinet this low is acceptable.

OK this seems to be working. Let's copy another 16 bars. This time we'll do it a slightly different way.

- Set the Locators between bars 33 and 49.
- Select the Parts [Edit>Select>Inside Locators] and Copy [Edit>Copy]. Make sure the Position Pointer is set to 49. 1. 1 and Paste [Edit> Paste] the Parts.

- Save song – compare with project5/7.arr.

Something new? I love pizzicato strings used to add that atmospheric touch. We will now add a simple arpeggio figure.

Take 5

- Select Track 5 (Ch 5) and rename it 'Pizzicato'.

Track Inspector
Output: USM
Program: 46
Patchname: Pizzicato Strings

Status Bar
Quantize [8]

Transport Bar
Locators: (L) 49.1.1 (R) 53.1.1
Activate AQ

- Record Take 5 (Figure 11.9).

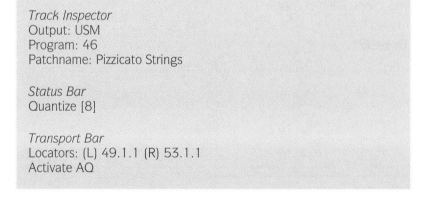

Figure 11.9 Record Take 5.

This figure is played at the beginning of the bar, just before the clarinet entry, and therefore avoids any confusion that may have resulted had we placed it elsewhere in the four measures cycle.

- Copy and Paste the pizzicato Part (bars 49 – 53) to bar 53. Glue the two Parts together.
- Copy and Paste the resulting Part to bar 57.
- Transpose that Part (bars 57 – 65) down a perfect fourth (–5).

Our canvas is filling up now and the stereo picture needs sorting out. We need not make any final decisions just yet, so let's use the Track Inspector to try out a few preliminary settings.

- Set the Locators between 49 and 65. Enable cycle and Play.
- Ensure no individual Parts are selected and using the Track Inspector, separate the two virtual guitarists by panning the first to L40 and the second to R40. Leave the strings in the centre. Place the clarinettist at L16 and the pizzicato strings at R16. We now have quite a nice spread.
- Set Locators – (L) 49.1.1 (R) 65.1.1 and Select all Parts [Edit>Select>Inside Locators] and Copy and Paste to bar 65.

- Save song – compare with project5/8.arr.

It's all going swimmingly so far and there's room on our canvas for more. Something nautical? A fragment from a well known sea shanty perhaps? *What Shall We Do With The Drunken Sailor* obviously! Played on the accordion of course!

Take 6

- Select Track 6 (Ch 6) and rename it 'Accordion'.

> *Track Inspector*
> Output: USM
> Program: 22
> Patchname: Accordion
>
> *Status Bar*
> Quantize [16]
>
> *Transport Bar*
> Locators: (L) 57.1.1 (R) 61.1.1
> Activate AQ

- Record Take 6 (Figure 11.10).

This fragment works best over the lower transposed section, hence the Locator positions of 57 – 61.

Figure 11.10 Record Take 6.

- What do we do with the drunken sailor? Dump him on the far left! – Track Inspector – Pan L64.
- Copy and Paste the accordion Part (bars 57 – 61) to bar 61. Glue the two Parts together.
- Copy and Paste the new accordion Part to bar 73.

- Save song – compare with project5/9.arr.

I think we've got room for a little more nautical nonsense. How about a Hornpipe?

Take 7

- Select Track 7 (Ch 7) and rename it 'Piccolo'

Track Inspector
Output: USM
Program: 73
Patchname: Piccolo

Status Bar
Quantize [16]

Transport Bar
Locators: (L) 64.1.1 (R) 66.1.1
Activate AQ

- Record Take 7 (Figure 11.11) – play one octave higher than written.

Figure 11.11 Record Take 7.

This fragment is placed at the end of the clarinet line and just before the pizzicato strings. No confusion.

- Copy the piccolo Part (bars 64 – 66) and Paste to bars 68, 72 and 76. We now have four piccolo Parts.
- Select the last two Parts (bars 72 – 74 and 76 – 78) and transpose them up a fifth by adding a value of 7 (7 semitones) in the Transpose Dialogue Box. I fancied a change!
- Where shall we place the piccolo player? Over on the right, away from the drunken sailor! – R63.

- Save song – compare with project5/10.arr.

At this point I think a couple of effects would work a treat at instilling yet more atmosphere to this backdrop. GM effects are not noted for their realism but, used carefully, in the background, they can work quite well. We can't use audio, because the brief specified MIDI for this project. Let's try the Seashore effect. Back to the top!

The Seashore effect – Program 123 on the GM sound set varies considerably from one sound module to another. I don't much like the USM version (could do without the seagulls!) but it serves our purpose.

Take 8

- Select Track 8 (Ch 8) and rename it 'Seashore'.

Track Inspector
Output: USM
Program: 123
Patchname: Seashore

Status Bar
Quantize [8]

Transport Bar
Locators: (L) 1.1.1 (R) 9.1.1
Activate AQ

Figure 11.12 Record Take 8.

- Record Take 8 (Figure 11.12).

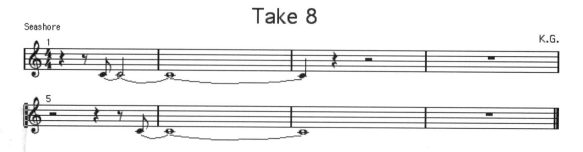

We'll leave it in the centre for now.

• Save song – compare with project5/11.arr.

Something else? A ship's bell perhaps. Ghostlike in the mist.

Take 9

• Select Track 9 (Ch 9) and rename it 'Tubular'.

Track Inspector
Output: USM
Program: 15
Patchname: Tubular Bells

Status Bar
Quantize [8]

Transport Bar
Locators: (L) 1.1.1 (R) 9.1.1
Activate AQ

• Record Take 9 (Figure 11.13).

Figure 11.13 Record Take 9.

• It works a treat. Pan it to R30 for now.
• Now we calculate how many times to repeat the Seashore and Tubular Bell. 72 bars, divided by 8 = 9 times. Use [Structure>Repeat Parts x9].

• Save song – compare with project5/12.arr.

What now? We have 80 bars of music, a full canvas with no room left for any moving parts without the risk of confusing the listener. I still think it needs something else. A pad of some kind. High strings in fifths will create a nice backdrop and sit well with the descending guitar chords.

Take 10

• Select Track 11 (Ch 11) and rename it 'Slow Strings'.

INFO

*N*ote we skipped Track 10 which is usually reserved for Drums when using General MIDI format.

Track Inspector
Output: USM
Program: 50
Patchname: String Ensemble 2

Status Bar
Quantize [4]

Transport Bar
Locators: (L) 1.1.1 (R) 9.1.1
Activate AQ

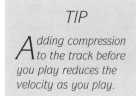

TIP

Adding compression to the track before you play reduces the velocity as you play.

- Record Figure 11.14 – play these gently. If you find it difficult to do so use the Compression Box in the Track Inspector. Try 50% or 75%. I have used 50% on mine.

Figure 11.14 Record Take 10.

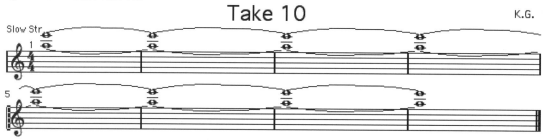

- Copy and Paste the Part (bars 1 – 9) to bar 9 [Structure>Repeat x1].
- Transpose the new Part (bars 9 – 17) down a perfect fourth (–5). Glue the two Parts together.
- Copy new Part (bars 1 – 7) to bar 17 until the end of the piece [Structure>Repeat Part(s) x4].
- To make the string line continuous we Select the Track and apply Legato [Functions>Legato].

- Save song – compare with project5/13.arr.

OK we have 80 bars, just over three minutes long. Time to end it. If used with a game it probably wouldn't need one. But what the hell! I like endings. We are going to add a very simple one note ending on the Guitar 1 Track.

Figure 11.15 Use compression if necessary.

Take 11

• Select Track 2 (Ch 2).

Status Bar
Quantize [4]

Transport Bar
Locators: (L) 81.1.1 (R) 83.1.1
Activate AQ

• Record Take 11 (Figure 11.16).

Figure 11.16 Record Take 11.

• Save song – compare with project5/14.arr.

The mix

Mixing this piece is straightforward enough. A label – KISS (Keep It Simple, Stupid) – is stuck to my monitor because it's easy to get carried away, especially with the comprehensive mixing facilities now available with Cubase VST, but I have learned through experience to use effects and signal processing sparingly.

Everybody does it differently, but I like to get the stereo picture and volume levels clear before I decide to add effects.

Up to now we have left Volume turned off on all Tracks in the Track Inspector (effectively all playing at 127). Before changing them I listened back and decided to alter the stereo picture slightly.

Guitar 1 actually functions as a kind of bass line. It's usual to place the bass in the centre so that's what I did. Guitar 2 was upsetting the balance a little. I moved it closer to the centre – R25 – and applied 75% compression. The clarinet was competing for space with the accordion, so I moved it to the right – R17. The pizzicato strings have changed sides – L16. They enter after the clarinet, which is on the right, and I wanted a contrast.

I used the MIDI Track Mixer to play around with the levels until I found a suitable balance. There is no automation so it was safe to do this.

See Figure 11.16(a) for an overall Track View.

A	M	C	T	Track	Chn	Pan		Vol		Cmp	Output
			♪	Guitar 1	1		<C>			53	OFF	Unive
			♪	Guitar 2	2		R25			53	75%	Unive
			♪	Strings	3		<C>			127	OFF	Unive
			♪	Clarinet	4		R17			60	OFF	Unive
			♪	Pizzicato	5		L16			97	OFF	Unive
			♪	Accordian	6		L64			74	OFF	Unive
			♪	Piccolo	7		R63			42	75%	Unive
			♪	Seashore	8		<C>			37	OFF	Unive
			♪	Tubular	9		R30			40	OFF	Unive
●			♪	Track 10	10		OFF			0	OFF	Unive
			♪	Slow Str.	11		<C>			35	50%	Unive

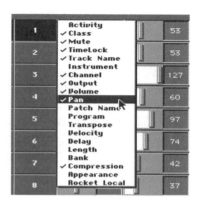

Track View and one of the drop-down menus.

Figure 11.17 VST Channel Mixer 2, View option 6 – 'VST Instruments only'.

Track Views are very useful for displaying several Track Parameters in an Arrangement at once. Click and hold on a Track column header and choose from the drop-down menu.

That settled, I listened again. The obvious candidate for Reverb was the Seashore sound. It needed more ambience. Instead of the seagulls sounding so close that they had come to pinch my sandwiches I wanted a more dreamy atmosphere. This is what I did.

I opened the VST Channel Mixer 2 [Panels>VST Channel Mixer 2].

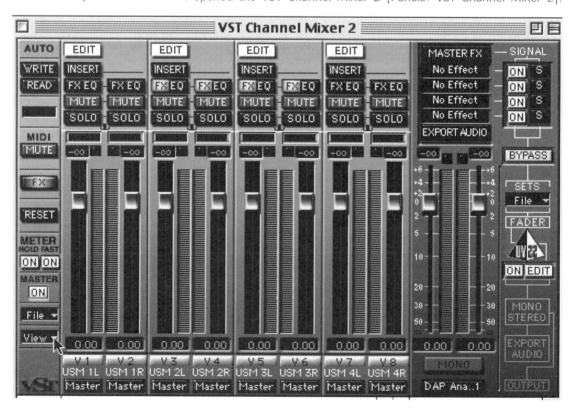

Clicking on the box marked 'View' I chose option 6 – 'VST Instruments only'. This gave me the four USM stereo outputs and the Master faders, shown in Figure 11.17.

I clicked on the blue button – on the left – marked FX and opened the VST Send Effects rack. I chose 'Reverb' from the first pop-up menu and the 'Long and Warm' preset from the second. I also ensured that the effect output was routed to 'Master' by checking the bus pop-up. (below the File pop-up).

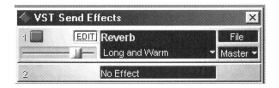

Figure 11.18 VST Send Effects rack

I opened the VST Instruments rack [Panel>VST Instruments], made sure Universal Sound was selected and active (the red button was lit), and pressed the 'Edit' button (Figure 11.19).

Figure 11.19 VST Instruments rack

This opened the Universal Sound Module Control Panel.

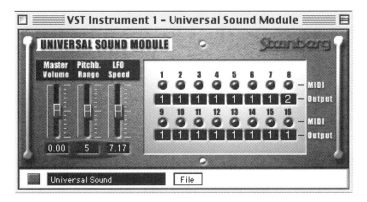

Figure 11.20 The USM Control Panel MIDI Channel 8 routed to Output 2.

The USM MIDI Outputs are set to 1 on all channels by default. The 'Seashore' is on Channel 8 and in order for me to treat it separately I changed its output to 2 in the pop up menu.

I returned to the VST Channel Mixer 2 and pressed the blue button marked FX at the top of the USM2 Channel Strip. This opened the VST Channel Settings Panel for USM2. I checked that 'Reverb' was selected in the pop up menu on Send No.1 Set the knob to around 1 o'clock. Activated the ON button (Figure 11.21).

Figure 11.21 VST Channel
Settings Panel – USM2

I pressed Play (on the Transport Bar) and returned to the VST Send Effects rack and adjusted the level 'on the fly', keeping it fairly high in this case (Figure 11.18).

I returned again to VST Channel Settings and using the Solo and Bypass buttons auditioned the Reverb (Figure 11.21).

None of the above took as long as it takes to read! It's quite easy when you get the hang of it.

Adding Reverb to the other tracks would, in my opinion, have made things muddy. Most of the sounds in the context of this piece sound fine. The pizzicato strings have been sampled with reverb anyway.

I decided the guitar would benefit from some judicious use of a chorus effect. All right, I know they didn't have digital effects processors back in Sir Francis Drake's day, but who cares! It serves our purpose of beefing things up a little. This what I did.

Opened VST Send Effects [Panel>VST Send Effects], added another effect processor and chose 'Chorus' from the first pop up menu and the Wide preset from the second. I also ensured that the effect output was routed to 'Master' by checking the bus pop-up (below the File pop-up) (Figure 11.22).

Figure 11.22 VST Send Effects
rack (chorus has been added).

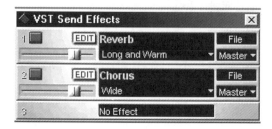

I clicked the 'Edit' button which gave me access to the Chorus Unit itself and set the Mix to 75% (Figure 11.23).

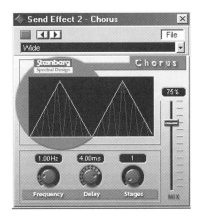

Figure 11.23 Send Effect 2 – Chorus

I opened the USM [Panels>VST Instruments] and pressed the 'Edit' button. This revealed the USM Control Panel. This time I routed Channels 1 and 2 (guitars) to Output 3 (Figure 11.24).

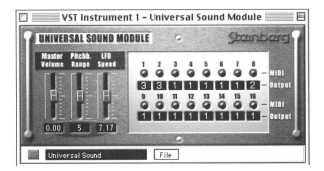

Figure 11.24 The USM Control Panel MIDI Channel 8 routed to Output 2. MIDI CHannels 1 and 2 routed to Channel 3.

I opened the VST Channel Mixer 2 [Panels>VST Channel Mixer 2] and pressed the blue button marked FX at the top of the USM3 Channel Strip. This opened the VST Channel Settings Panel for USM3 (Figure 11.25).

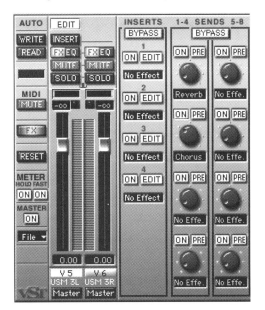

Figure 11.25 VST Channel Settings – USM3.

After ensuring that 'Chorus' was selected in the pop-up box for Send 2, set the knob to about 10 o'clock and activated the ON button.

I pressed Play (on the Transport Bar) and returned to the VST Send Effects rack and adjusted the level 'on the fly', keeping it fairly high in this case.

Returned again to VST Channel Settings and using the SOLO and BYPASS buttons auditioned the Chorused guitars. Adjusted the Send No.2 knob a little.

Load Song File project5/project5.all and have a listen. Open the VST Channel Mixer 2 and Send Effects from the Panels menu and have a look around. The Volume levels can be seen in the MIDI Track Mixer (Figure 11.26).

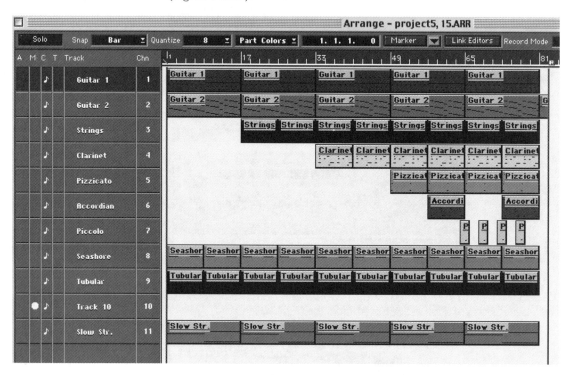

Figure 11.26 Project5.all –
Arrange window view.

The result? I'm happy. There's always another way to do it and another possible mix but part of doing this kind of thing for a living is deciding when to stop. Time's money. Commitments have to be made. No doubt you would do it another way. Go ahead! Experiment with the mix. That's how you learn but don't even think about altering it and claiming copyright – I have a brilliant lawyer!

A look at musical form

12

To examine the Cubase files for this chapter, from the CD, copy the folders named 'form' and 'exile' to your computer.

Practically all music has form; a structure or framework, often planned before the composition process even begins. I'm referring here to composed music as opposed to improvised music (although improvisation is often based on form anyway). The casual listener does not always notice the form, nor should they because in most cases it's a hidden element. They enjoy the music on a superficial level, and quite rightly so. After all, when we gaze at a work of art we are not necessarily examining its hidden form. We appreciate the whole picture.

Sometimes the musical form is very simple and glaringly obvious, the 12 bar blues being a perfect example. Other times it's very complicated and stretched across a long time span. A classical symphony, for instance, may contain four complete movements and last up to 45 minutes or more.

One thing's for sure. Although the listener may not be consciously aware of musical form they certainly know when it's missing! Formless music – and plenty has been composed and forgotten – lacks the sense of completeness which is perceived by the listener and held in the memory. Of course good music has been written without conventional musical form but it has no place in this book which is primarily concerned with producing commercial music.

Form can be anything you want it to be. It's about organization. However, over time, certain musical forms have appeared and remained embedded in popular culture. They've stood the test of time and provided a basic structure for composers to use repeatedly. Let's take a quick look at some established musical forms in three very different genres.

Simple three part forms

A simple three part form is referred to as ABA. The third section is a recapitulation of the first, sometimes harmonically and melodically modified. The middle section is a contrast to avoid monotony. The next extract is from a Haydn Piano Sonata (Figure 12.1).

- Load form/form.all/haydn.arr and view the Arrange window (Figure 12.2).
- Set the Output columns to the Universal Sound Module

Track 1 contains the right hand Parts and Track 2 the left. You will

INFO

Recapitulation – posh word for repetition!

TIP

Remember that Arrangements (.arr) contained in a Song file (.all) can be opened from the Windows menu. [Windows> Arrangements].

Figure 12.1 haydn.arr –
Score view.

notice that the Marker Track contains a reference to the form (Figure
12.2). Section A is 16 bars long. It is in fact an eight bar segment
played twice.

Figure 12.2 haydn.arr –
haydn.arr – Arrange
window view.

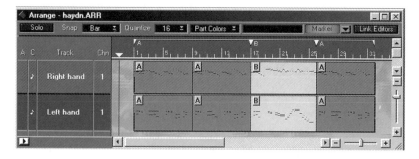

An analogy: think of A as the Home page on a themed Internet site.
B is a contrasting section and consists of nine measures. The rhythmic
structure and phrasing are similar to the A section but the harmony sets
it apart. The scenery is familiar but we've definitely left the Home page.
The piece finishes with a note for note repetition of A. Back Home! It
would be more accurately described as an AABA structure.

Figure 12.3 minuet.arr – Score view.

- Here's another example – form/form.all/minuet.arr – this time from Bach's French Suite (Figure 12.3).
- Set the Output columns to the Universal Sound Module

Again we have the A section followed by a contrasting B section. However, in this example the recapitulation has been varied. The reason? Well A ends on the dominant and sounds incomplete. Bach needed an ending. He begins the recapitulation the same (for two bars) but then leads us home to the tonic in the last bar. The Marker Track shows this structure as A1 B and A2.

Jazz standards

Jazz musicians often use the classic standard song repertoire from the first half of the 20th century for their improvisations. 'I Got Rhythm' by Gershwin is a typical example. Although in a completely different style from the minuet, its form is basically the same; AABA. Here's a tune in a similar style called 'Raising Standards'.

Figure 12.4 raisings.arr –
Arrange window view.

- Load form/form.all/raisings.arr (Figure 12.4).
- Set the Output columns to the Universal Sound Module.

Ensure that the General MIDI Drum Map has been loaded [File>Open from Library>General MIDI Drum Map].

The Marker Track shows the form. Section A1 and A2 are both eight bars long. The difference between them lies in bars 15 and 16, in the A2 section, where the melody and harmony have been modified. Section B is a contrasting section, generally referred to, by jazz musicians, as the 'bridge'. The tune finishes with eight bars of A3. Again things have been changed slightly to bring about the ending.

Pop songs

Pop songs are varied in their structure. However one form seems to be more predominant than most. A verse followed by a chorus is repeated two or three times and contrasted with a bridge. This gives way once again to the verse and chorus. Sometimes the bridge is used again. This corresponds to an ABABCAB structure. Here's an example.

- Load exile/exile.all/exile.arr and view the Arrange window.
- Set the Output columns to the Universal Sound Module.

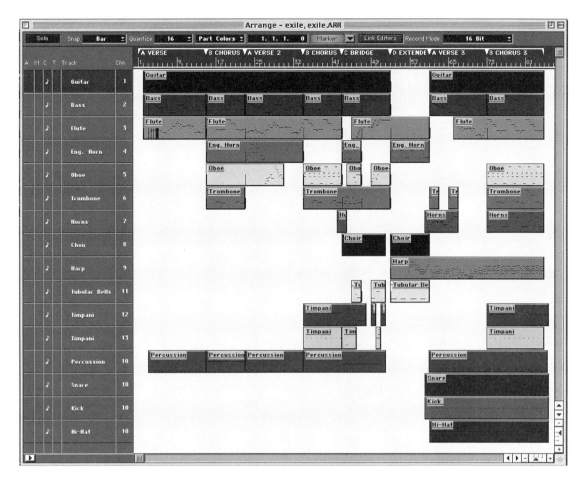

This tune, although an instrumental, follows the format of many a rock song in its construction. Medieval in character it could have been played by an electric folk band from the 70s such as Fairport Convention.

It kicks off with a verse (A) lasting 14 bars followed by an eight bar chorus (B). The verse and chorus are then repeated. This takes us up to bar 42. To repeat things again would be bordering on the tedious so a 10 bar bridge is introduced for relief (C). Now that could have led straight back to either the verse or chorus, (as it does in millions of songs) but in this case the bridge has been extended by adding another eight bar section (D). This helps build a sense of expectancy. The verse returns and is followed by a chorus and ending. What we have then is a ABABCDAB structure.

It's a good idea to have a basic form in mind before starting a composition. Although you will probably modify it as you write the piece, jotting down a simple structure first will serve as a guide.

Figure 12.5 exile.arr – Arrange window view.

13 The building blocks of composition

To examine the Cubase files for this chapter: From the CD, copy the folders named 'exile' and 'blocks' to your computer.

In Chapter 2 I explained how 'technically challenged' keyboard players, like myself, can record a difficult piece of music by breaking it up into manageable chunks. We dismantle the composition, piece by piece and rebuild it again as Parts on a Track in the Arrange window within Cubase VST. You could liken this process to a building being dismantled and reassembled, brick by brick, in a new location. There is much to be learned by doing this, and Cubase VST is an ideal place to do it because we can see the constituent parts, or building blocks, of a composition clearly displayed on the Arrange window.

The phrase

You probably discovered earlier, when sequencing three completely different styles of music, that musical common sense prompted you to play and record the music as complete phrases. We can assume then that a phrase is the smallest structural unit used for composition. It has a sense of completeness. It can be sung or played in a single breath and has a definite beginning and ending.

- Load exile/exile.all/exile.arr and view the flute (Track 3) in the Score Editor.
- Set the Output columns to the Universal Sound Module.

The first phrase is coloured red. It's a complete unit. Think of it as a musical sentence. Better still, think of it as a musical question. It's followed by another phrase, the answer, marked blue. After this there are two more question and answer phrases. Look through and play the score to identify other such phrases. I've marked a few to get you going.

What do these phrases consist of? What is the main ingredient? Well melody for a start. For me, this is usually the most important part of the creative process. The melody comes first and the rest follows later.

Melody

OK, not all music relies on melody, but the overwhelming majority does. How many times have you heard a snatch of melody and it's instant recall time? You know exactly where it came from. Even if you can't remember where its origins lie, the damn thing nags you silly until you eventually find out. That's the power of melody. That recall – depending on how old you are! – will often bring to mind a particular memory. It may well bring submerged emotions to the surface. Powerful stuff!

What constitutes a melody? At its most basic; a string of notes which rise and fall. But that's not enough.

- Load blocks/blocks.all/oddnotes.arr (Figure 13.1).
- Set the Output column to the Universal Sound Module.

oddnotes.arr

Listen to this group of notes. Not very memorable, is it?

Figure 13.1 A string of notes that rise and fall ...

- Now load blocks/blocks.all/igetit.arr (Figure 13.2).
- Set the Output column to the Universal Sound Module.

igetit.arr

Mozart

Figure 13.2 ...are transformed into melody.

It's the same order of notes, but what a transformation. It's instantly recognizable as 'Eine Kleine Nacht Musik' by Mozart, an absolute master of melody. What brought about the transformation? The rhythm. Without a rhythmic shape the melody does not exist.

What else? A distinctive shape, brought about by the pitch of the notes as a melody unfolds. A string of adjacent notes soon becomes monotonous without a leap – large or small, up or down – of some kind.

Take another look at the first few phrases of 'Exile' (exile/exile.all/exile.arr). Now this is a gentle melody, nothing very dramatic, which gradually climbs a scale. To make it a little more interesting there is a leap of a fourth between the first two notes (A and D). Each time the melody climbs a step there is a return to the A before leaping back up again and continuing the ascent.

High climax points within the melodic shape are also important for emotional intensity. In this case the highest note arrives at the beginning of each chorus (high E – marked purple).

Low notes can have the opposite effect and are often used to calm things down. The English Horn does just that between bars 53 and 61 (Track 4).

A good melody can be likened to well written prose. A readable page of text contains clearly defined phrases and frequent use of punctuation. Bear this in mind when writing melodies. Time taken crafting a memorable melody is time well spent. More on this in Chapter 14.

Harmony

This is a vast subject which needs a complete book of its own. In fact there are several excellent books available. If you're into composing and arranging – you must be if you bought this book – I'm assuming that you already have a basic knowledge of the subject. However, I can supply a few guidelines.

Beginner composers working with Cubase or similar sequencers often make the mistake of trying to write a melody and harmony together. It doesn't usually work! Not many people can control both elements at once, not least a beginner. The usual result of this way of writing is either a few measures of block chords following every single melody note with the bass playing only root notes or a few measures of repetitive chords and a boring melody line. Everything grinds to a halt pretty soon afterwards. It's a very common mistake and simply the result of trying to think of two things (sometimes three if rhythm is included) at once.

It's far easier to get the melody down first. It's what people are going to remember after all. Craft the melody, make it interesting, and add chords afterwards. You will discover that a melody often suggests the harmony anyway.

It depends on the style of music of course, but when you add the harmony, avoid having all the chords in root position. There's an absolute wealth of possibilities available to us by just using very simple diatonic chords. The secret lies in using the inversions. Here's just some of what is available (Figure 13.3). Using just a C scale and first and second inversions we have a choice of 21 chords, and that's without adding the seventh and sixth.

> *D*iatonic chords are built using notes from the prevailing key of the moment. e.g. the chords in Figure 13.3 use only notes from the C major scale – C major being the prevailing key.

* Load blocks/blocks.all/triads.arr to hear and view them.
* Set the Output column to the Universal Sound Module.

Diatonic Triads

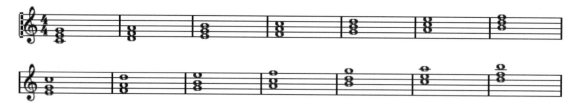

Figure 13.3 The secret lies in using inversions.

That's all very well', I hear you say, 'I play guitar and know a lot of chords, but my knowledge of harmony is limited. It would take me hours to work out the correct voicing.'

Don't worry. Keep writing. You will learn as you go. One way to get a more interesting harmonic structure is through careful construction of the bass line. Make it distinctive. Give it a life of its own and, where possible, and appropriate, have it move in the opposite direction to the melody. This will nearly always give a good result. This movement inevitably provides interesting inversions and passing notes.

- Load exile/exile.all/dullbass.arr and play it through.
- Set the Output columns to the Universal Sound Module.

The guitar is playing this chord sequence:

Dm / A7 / | Dm / / / | Dm / A7 / | Dm / / / |

F / Gm / | Am / / / | C / E7 / | Am / / / ||

The chords are OK, simple yes, but it's a rather plaintive melody and doesn't need complicated chords. Not quite right though, is it? How can we make it more harmonically interesting?

- Switch to exile/exile.all/exile.arr and play the opening measures.

By having the bass move, for the most part, in the opposite direction to the melody we have created the following:

Dm / A7 / | Dm7 / / Bbmaj7 | Dm / A7 / | Dm / / Gm9 |
   C#   C   A

F / Gm7 / | Fmaj7 / / / | C / E7 / | Am / Am / ||
   F   B   C

That's better. The bass is now playing a kind of counter melody – appropriate here because the drums have yet to enter – and creates several inversions, new chords and interesting passing notes along the way.

Modulation is another way to make the harmonic structure interesting. It's often best to write what the melody suggests and the modulation should be smooth and natural sounding. The listener will not consciously perceive these key changes – but their subconscious will.

'Exile' (exile/exile.all/exile.arr) is a simple enough song but it's helped along the way with several key changes. You can see them indicated in the Marker Track:

The verse is in D minor, the chorus in G minor and the bridge uses D flat major and A major. The bridge extension returns to D minor. These modulations are the direct result of the melody. Not the other way around.

Rhythm

Another vast subject. We have seen how a rhythmic design can change an ordinary string of notes into a memorable tune. Its most important role though is in the accompaniment. It can probably be best studied in piano music, where it is usually evident in the left hand part.

Most instrumental music used in the commercial world makes extensive use of rhythm in the accompaniment, usually drums and percussion, and is often derived from the character of the melody. For example, I wrote the melody for 'Exile' (exile/exile.all/exile.arr) before adding rhythm and harmony. The melody suggested both.

Take another look at the melody in the beginning phrase and you will

INFO

*M*odulation is the changing from one key to another within a composition.

Figure 13.4 A classic rock drum rhythm – Score Edit view.

notice that the first nine notes are 1/8th notes (quavers). Pretty straightforward stuff, that, to my ears, suggested a classic rock drum rhythm (Figure 13.4) used on countless recordings over the last four or five decades:

Eighth notes on a closed hi-hat – snare drum on the second and fourth beats of each measure – and kick drum on the first, second half of second, and third beats. Simple but effective (view the Drum Tracks in the Drum or Score Editors – Figures 13.5 and 13.6). Of course we all hear things differently and had that melody been written by someone else (you?) the rhythmic scheme may well have taken a different turn.

Figure 13.5 A classic rock drum rhythm – Drum Edit view

Figure 13.6 A classic rock drum rhythm – Key Edit view

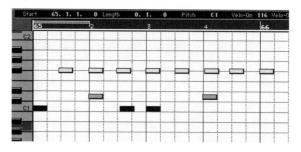

Of course rhythmic accompaniment need not be restricted solely to drums. It is very easy to create rhythm in Cubase without the use of percussion sounds. Rhythm can be generated with absolute accuracy using synthesized sounds to play arpeggios and other percussive patterns. These take on a more pulsating effect than the humanly played equivalent. For example: in 'Exile' (exile/exile.all/exile.arr) the drums don't appear until the third verse. However an eighth note pulse has been implied by the guitar arpeggios (Track 1) which also happen to supply the harmony. This is reinforced by a sixteenth note arpeggio pattern played by the harp (Track 9) on the last verse and chorus.

Techno and dance music are playing an increasing role in music for the media. Melody is a secondary consideration in this style of music and the composition process would probably start from the bottom up, with rhythmic patterns and loops being created first. More on this in Chapter 21.

Melody making 14

To examine the Cubase files for this chapter: from the CD, copy the folders named 'cells' and 'exile' to your computer.

Memorable melody – how's it done?

In the previous chapter we used small melodic fragments to build a kind of musical collage suitable for background use. The fragments remained undeveloped. We'll now have a look at how small fragments of melody can be expanded into larger structures. In other words we will construct a melody.

'Construct a melody!' I can hear you saying, 'surely melodies aren't constructed but revealed, in moments of divine inspiration, to extremely gifted musical people like, Mozart, Irving Berlin, Lennon and McCartney and the like. Not ordinary people like us.

'Not so. The first ideas are often inspirational but the hard work of building and constructing soon takes over. As usual it's 1% brain wave, 99% hard slog. So you're in with a chance.

'So how is it done? Well there are no hard and fast rules. However, there are some guidelines and general principles that have worked well over the last few hundred years or so. Why do we remember certain melodies, and not others? In most cases we remember the well crafted ones that are carefully developed from a few distinctive ideas. These ideas, are then repeated and varied to form a complete melody. The two key ingredients are repetition and variation. Without repetition the listener has nothing to hold on to and soon becomes bewildered. Without variation boredom sets in.

Single cell construction

Don't be frightened of repetition. Without it nobody will be likely to remember anything you compose. A good way of getting started on developing and constructing melodies is to write a short motif or phrase, repeat it several times and introduce variations in pitch. Figure 14.1 shows a melody constructed this way.

After creating a short motif, I duplicated it five times and varied the pitches of the notes each time to form a continuous flowing melody. I used several Tracks, for clarity, but of course, it could all be done on a single Track!

Figure 14.1 Single cell
construction – Arrange window
view

Figure 14.1 Single cell
construction – Arrange window
view

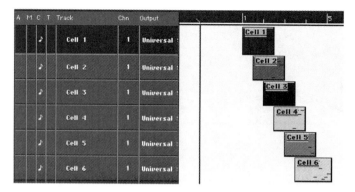

Figure 14.2 Single cell
construction – Score view.

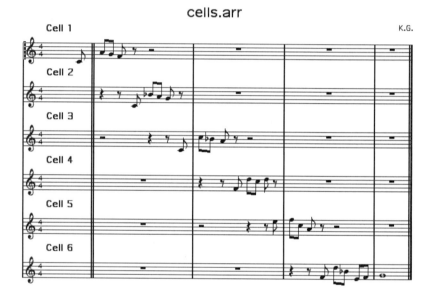

- Load cells/cells.all and follow it through.
- Set the Output columns to the Universal Sound Module.

- Cell 1 – cells.all/cell1.arr – the so called inspirational beginning. Although it ends on the tonic (we are in the key of F) it has an air of expectancy about it which suggests continuation.
- Cell 2 – cells.all/cell2.arr – by raising the pitch of all but the first note I was able to create a new phrase. The air of expectancy continues. We are climbing.
- Cell 3 – cells.all/cell3.arr – another copy is added. The pitches are raised and the climbing continues.
- Cell 4 – cells.all/cell4.arr – ... and continues
- Cell 5 – cells.all/cell5.arr – we begin a descent.
- Cell 6 – cells.all/cell6.arr – this time the motif is extended to complete a musical sentence.

Musical questions and answers

Another way of developing melody is to create musical statements that suggest an answer. The melody for 'Exile' was constructed this way.

- Take a look at the begriming of the Flute Part in 'Exile' (exile/exile.all/exile.arr).
- Set the Output columns to the Universal Sound Module.

The opening phrase (marked red) poses a kind of musical question that begs an answer. We'll call it Q1. The answer follows in the next phrase (marked blue). We'll call it A1. Although different to Q1 – note how it rises higher in response – the last five notes are a recall of the last five notes of Q1. Already we have repetition with a slight variation.

The next phrase (again in red – call it Q2) follows the same rhythmic pattern as Q1 but the notes are completely different. That air of expectancy has been fulfilled and a new question asked. A2 the next phrase (in blue) again answers the question and is a varied repetition of A1.

All this often comes naturally, without thinking. We have merely analysed it. However, if you're stuck for ideas, this is a sure fire method of keeping things moving. There are so many ways to achieve this onward flow that a whole book is needed on the subject. You can though, learn a great deal by taking time to listen and analyse other melodies in this way. Reading music, although helpful, is not always necessary.

Figure 14.3 A way of developing melody – questions and answers.

15

Audio recording – the basics

The next project in the book incorporates the use of a pre-recorded Audio Track containing an improvised saxophone solo behind the main tune. This can be replaced with another instrument or a vocal track. At this point then, it seems appropriate to have a quick look at the basic audio recording procedure and microphone techniques needed to do this. If you don't happen to play an acoustic instrument and can't stand to hear the sound of your own voice use a synthesized sound instead!

Recording vocals

To record vocals a directional mic mounted on a stand is the usual method and the singer will most likely be standing. If you have a wobbly wooden floor, isolate the stand from the floor to prevent low frequency rumble travelling up the mic stand and on to your recordings. If you can afford it, a condenser mic is best, but a dynamic mic such as the trusty Shure SM57 or SM58 will still produce good results.

Although most vocal mics have built-in wind shields it is still a good idea to use a pop screen. There are several types on the market these days. The DIY alternative, a pair of tights stretched over a bent wire coat hanger does the same job. Apart from preventing sudden pops, if you are recording a vocalist other than yourself, it will also prevent them getting too close to the microphone.

A distance of between 15 and 60 cm between the mouth and microphone is usual, depending on the strength and character of the vocalist, with the mic tilted slightly, either up or down, away from a direct line with the mouth. A greater distance is fine but bear in mind the fact that more gain may be needed and if the vocalist has a quiet voice problems with noise could arise. Keep the mic away from reflective surfaces, walls being an obvious example.

Recording electric guitars

A dynamic mic such as the Shure SM58 is the usual choice for the job. To begin with place it between 15 and 30 cm from the centre of one of the speakers in the amp cabinet. Experiment by moving it off centre from there to alter the tone. Try using two mics, one further away or at the side, or even behind the speaker cabinet. Use a similar method for bass guitar, but place it further away to avoid a boxy sound.

Recording acoustic guitars

A directional mic is best, preferably a condenser type, however reasonably good results can still be achieved with a dynamic mic. Position it about 45 cms from the sound hole. Avoid the temptation to place it any closer unless you want a boomy sound!

Recording brass and woodwind

The SM58 will do fine, but a better choice is a condenser mic. Where you place the mic depends very much on where most of the sound comes from, saxes and brass from the bell, flute from the mouthpiece etc. However, particularly with woodwind, the sound emanates from other parts of the instrument and it is better therefore to keep the mic at a reasonable distance from the player, 45 cms or so is usually OK.

Recording strings

Treat individual stringed instruments such as violin in the same way as the acoustic guitar. If you are fortunate enough to have the space and are recording a small string ensemble, use two mics suspended above the players mounted at right angles to each other for a good stereo image.

From microphone to audio Track – the signal route

OK you are all set to record that blistering solo but how do you actually get the audio signal onto a Cubase Audio Track? If you are new to recording and find it confusing, here's a summary of the main things to do.

* Connect the audio signal from your external mixer to the audio card input.
* Open VST Inputs [Panel>VST Inputs] and ensure that the inputs of your audio card are activated (Figure 15.1).

Figure 15.2 Open the audio Track Inspector.

Figure 15.1 Ensure that the audio card inputs are active.

* In the Arrange window, select an audio Track and open the Track Inspector (Figure 15.2).
* Click on the right hand side of the Input button and select either IN 1 L or IN 1 R.
* Click on the left hand side to activate it.
* Open the VST Channel Mixer [Panels>VST Channel Mixer 1]. The Input button at the top of the fader strip should now be illuminated (it corresponds with the Input button in the Track Inspector). If it isn't, activate it (Figure 15.3).
* Activate the tiny 'In' button above the level meter. This allows you to visually monitor the incoming audio signal (Figure 15.4).

- Adjust the input level using your external mixer or your sound card's software mixer.
- Record the audio using the Transport Bar as you do with MIDI Tracks.

This process is outlined again in Project 6, when a saxophone solo is actually recorded.

Figure 15.3 (left) The VST Channel Mixer – the Input button is illuminated.

Figure 15.4 (right) Activate the 'In' button to monitor the incoming audio signal.

Project 6 — a football theme

16

Musical objectives

- Decide upon a suitable lead instrument to carry the melody in keeping with the musical demands of the brief.
- Construct a melody from a small melodic 'cell' by applying repetition and pitch variation.
- Compose a rhythmic bass part to compliment the newly invented melody and consider the harmonic possibilities this implies.
- Use 3 part sectional harmony to build a 'brass section'.
- Use Tenor Sax or other instrument to provide an improvised solo behind the main melody.

New Cubase skills

- Use Logical Edit to lengthen a selected group of notes.
- Create, name and record an Audio Track
- Use the Track Inspector to select an Audio Input, choose Track Status and Enable record mode – mono/stereo
- Use the VST Channel Mixer 1 to verify input signal, check and adjust audio signal input levels.
- Use the Transport Bar to set up a drop-in/drop-out recording region.
- Use the VST Channel Mixer Settings to apply Dynamic Processor – Soft Clip – to the recorded audio signal.

Preparation

- From the CD, copy the folder named 'project6' to your computer.
- On your computer create a folder called 'mywork6' or something similar in which to save your work.
- Open a New Arrangement [File>New Arrangement].
- On the Transport Bar, set the Time Signature to 4/4.
- Our tempo for this piece is 140 bpm. Set this in the Mastertrack [Edit>List>Mastertrack/Graphical Mastertrack].
- From the CD, copy the project6 folder to your computer's desktop or other location.
- In the 'mywork6' folder, save as Song File – myproj6.all or something similar.

The brief

You have been commissioned to compose a 1 minute theme for a football program. It must be upbeat in tempo, attention grabbing, and uplifting in character.

To gain an overall picture, at this point you may prefer to listen to the finished thing rather than let things unfold. To do so, load project6/project6.all.

As always, you will need to set the Output columns to the VST Instruments called Universal Sound Module and LM-9 otherwise you may not hear anything! (See the Appendix – Page 194 – for details.)

Take 1

- Create a new Track [Structure>Create Track] (Ch 1) and rename it 'Brass 1'.

Track Inspector
Output: USM
Program: 62
Patchname: Brass Section

Status Bar
Quantize [8]

Transport Bar
(L) 1.1.1 (R) 3.1.1
Activate AQ

- A blank Arrange page presents a daunting prospect. But wait – an initial fragment of melody has presented itself and stubbornly sticks in the mind, refusing to go away (Figure 16.1). Let's record it and take it from there. Choose Quantize Type Groove: 2)8th+8 from the Functions menu. I've chosen a Brass Synth sound to get that 'uplifting' quality.

Figure 16.1 Take 1 – A fragment of melody comes to mind.

Figure 16.1a Choose Quantize Type Groove: 2) 8th+8 from the Functions menu.

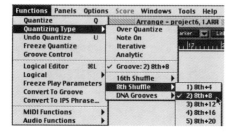

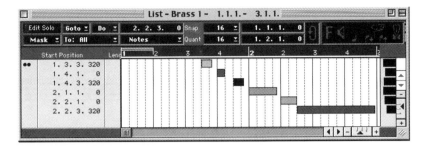

Figure 16.2 Groove:2) 8th+8
– off-beat eighth notes are
delayed by 320 ticks.

The result of the chosen groove can be seen in the List Edit window. Note how all the off-beat eighth notes are delayed by 320 ticks (Figure 16.2).

• Save song – compare with project6/1.arr.

When loading *my* Cubase Arrange files into *your* Song file version for comparison, remember to:

1 Check that the Universal Sound Module and any other VST Instruments needed have been loaded.
2 Ensure the Output columns display the USM and any other VST Instruments needed.
3 To avoid confusion, close down *my* Arrange file version before any further saving of *your* Song file.

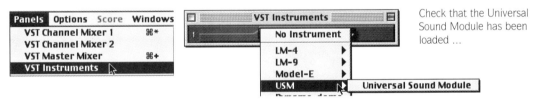

Check that the Universal
Sound Module has been
loaded ...

... and ensure the Output
columns display the USM.

The plan here is to construct a theme by repeating this fragment and applying variation to it in the various Editors.

• Repeat the Part seven times [Structure>Repeat Parts>x7]. We now have a 16 bar section comprised of eight two-bar Parts to work on. I shall refer to these Parts as Cells 1 – 8 (Figure 16.3).

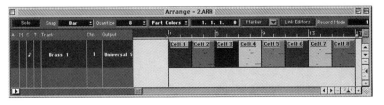

Figure 16.3 Cells 1 – 8 in the
Arrange window.

Here's what we do (Figure 16.4):

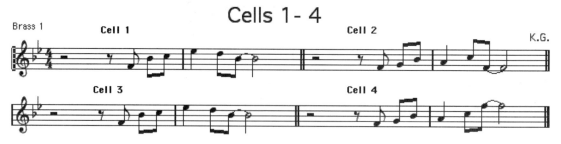

Figure 16.4 Cells 1 – 4; by keeping the rhythmic framework intact and altering the pitch of the notes, we generate melody.

- Cell 1: bars (1 – 3) Although it ends on the tonic (we are in the key of Bb) it definitely suggests continuation so …
- Cell 2: (bars 3 – 5) By keeping the rhythmic framework of Cell 1 intact and altering the pitch of the notes we generate more melody. Alter the pitch of the notes as shown by using either the Score or Key Editors.

Changing the notes by dragging will destroy our chosen Quantize Type and snap them to the selected Quantize option shown on the Status Bar, so before you leave the Editor, ensure 8 is shown as the selected Quantization on the Status Bar, that Groove: 2)8th+8 is chosen, and press 'Q' on your keyboard to re-quantize the Part. A better method is to change the notes on the Status Bar itself (left), which will retain their quantized position. This is a safer way of working.

TIP

To avoid changing a note's position when altering the pitch use the Status Bar in preference to dragging it.

- Cell 3: (bars 5 – 7) The initial phrase can be repeated again without risk of boredom so leave it untouched.
- Cell 4: (bars 7 – 9) We use the same note pattern as Cell 2 but raise the last note by an octave. This really does suggest continuation. Upwards! The brief stated uplifting, remember.
- Save song – compare with project6/2.arr.

- Save song.

We continue with Cells 5 – 8 (Figure 16.5).

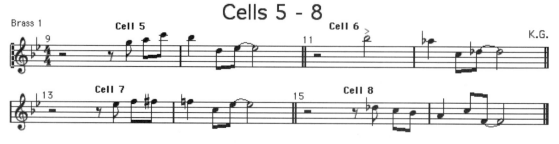

Figure 16.5 Cells 5 – 8; note the change in Cell 6.

- Cell 5: (bars 9 – 11) We change the notes to continue the ascent to C and have the melody fall from there.
- Cell 6: (bars 11 – 13) Our listeners are unconsciously expecting yet another fall in pitch and a repetition of the familiar rhythmic pattern, but this time we surprise them by applying the brakes. We delete the

first three notes – in the Score or Key Editors – and replace them with a half note (minim) half a beat earlier than expected, and continue the descent.

- Cell 7: (bars 13 – 15) We hover around a bit ...
- Cell 8: (bars 15 – 17) ... before landing back on the note F, where we began.

- Save song – compare with project6/3.arr.

Using Logical Edit

Play it through. I think the last note in each cell should be a bit longer by a couple of beats. Now we could go through the whole thing and lengthen the notes manually, but that's tedious. Instead we are going to use that most frightening of Cubase features, the Logical Editor, to do them all in one fell swoop. Here goes!

- In the Arrange window, select the Track and open either the Score or Key Editor.
- Open the Logical Editor [Functions>Logical Editor]. If you haven't used it before it will probably open in Easy mode by default. Forget that! Choose the Expert mode; (the button is down near the bottom right hand corner). We are going in at the deep end!

The eight notes we need to lengthen (one in each Part or cell) are all exactly the same length because we duplicated them. In my example this length is 9.2824 (the 9 represents nine sixteenth notes) but will almost certainly be slightly different in yours. I am going to lengthen them by seven sixteenth notes. The lowest note is F3 and the highest is F4 (Figure 16.6).

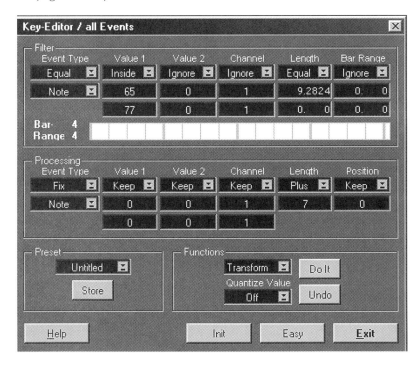

Figure 16.6 The Logical Editor – all the notes between F3/65 and F4/77 are lengthened by seven sixteenth notes.

There are two main sections to the Logical Editor:

1 Filter – where we select events to change.
2 Processing – where the selected events are changed.

• Initialize with the Init button (lower right hand corner) and working from left to right in the Filter section:

• In the Event Type boxes select Equal and Note (left).

• In the Value 1 boxes choose Inside and scroll the top value to 65/F3 and the lower to 77/F4.

• In the Value 2 and Channel boxes select Ignore.

• In the Length boxes enter Equal and the value of the note we need to alter (in my case 9.2824).

TIP

Working in the Logical Editor from another Editor gives you the option to abort the process should you not like the result.

• In the Bar Range boxes select Ignore.

Working from left to right in the Processing section:

• In the Event Type boxes select Fix and Note.

• In the Value 1, 2 and Channel boxes select Keep.

• In the Length boxes select Plus and enter the value to add in the lower
  (in my case 7.0 – seven sixteenth notes)..

• In the Position box select Keep.

• Press the Do It button.

You have now successfully changed eight things at once in a matter of
moments. Well that's the theory anyway.
    What we actually told Logical Editor to do was:

1   (Filter section) Find all notes between 65/F3 and 77/F4 that are
    9.2824 in length and,
2   (Processing section) Lengthen those notes by seven (sixteenth notes).

Using the Logical Editor will become quicker in time, I promise! It really
does save a great deal of time.

• In the Arrange window, with the Pencil Tool, lengthen the last Part
  (bars 15 – 17) by one bar to accommodate the longer note we have
  just created and glue all the Parts together.

• Save song – compare with project6/4.arr.

What next? It obviously needs a pretty lively rhythm but all I can hear at the moment (mentally) is a four to the bar 'Dance Style' bass drum of some kind.

Take 2

- Create a new MIDI Track [Structure>Create Track] (Ch 10) and rename it 'Kick Drum'.
- Ensure the General MIDI Drum Map is loaded [File>Open from Library>General MIDI Drum Map].

Track Inspector
Output: LM-9
Patchname: Beat Box

Status Bar
[Quantize 8]

Transport Bar
Locators: (L) 2.1.1 (R) 6.1.1
Activate AQ

- Record four bars of kick drum (C1) (Figure 16.7) and copy the Part three times to complete 16 bars.

Figure 16.7 Take 2 – record four bars of Kick Drum.

- Save song – compare with project6/5.arr.

A bass line is needed. Because of the drum machine style kick drum, a bass synth sound suggests itself. Repeated eighth notes maybe?

Take 3

Place cursor on Track 1, create a new MIDI Track [Structure>Create Track] (Ch 2) and rename it 'Bass'.

Track Inspector
Output: USM
Program: 40
Patchname: Synth Bass 2
Transpose −12

Status Bar
Quantize [8]

Transport Bar
(L) 2.1.1 (R) 18.1.1
Activate AQ

- Using the same Quantize Type as the Brass Track – Groove: 2)8th+8 – record the 16 bars between the Locators (Figure 16.8). Breaking it down into four bar cycles is probably the easiest way. Note bars 6 – 10 are a repeat of bars 2 – 6, so copying that will save time.

Figure 16.8 Take 3 – record 16 bars of Synth Bass 2.

The choice of notes for the first eight bars (2 – 10) is pretty straight-forward stuff. Tonic to dominant etc. Things get more interesting in bars 10 – 16 where chromatic movement is beginning to suggest more adventurous harmony.

- Save song – compare with project6/6.arr.

Take 4

- Create a new MIDI Track (Ch 3) and rename it 'Brass 2'.

Track Inspector
Output: USM
Program: 62
Patchname: Brass Section

Status Bar
Quantize [8]

Transport Bar
Locators: (L) 2.1.1 (R) 18.1.1
Activate AQ

TIP

Writing the bass line and melody will often suggest interesting harmony that may never have occurred had the chords been worked on first.

- Using Groove: 2) 8th+8 record the 16 bars between the Locators (Figure 16.9). Break it down if necessary. It's a harmony part and we will examine it closer after the next Track is recorded.
- Save song – compare with project6/7.arr.

Figure 16.9 Take 4 – record 16 bars of Brass 2.

Take 5

- Create a new MIDI Track (Ch 4) and rename it 'Brass 3'.

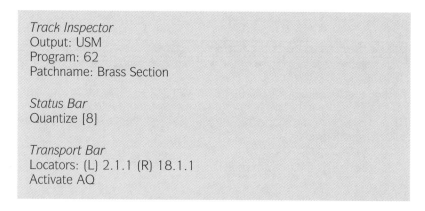

Track Inspector
Output: USM
Program: 62
Patchname: Brass Section

Status Bar
Quantize [8]

Transport Bar
Locators: (L) 2.1.1 (R) 18.1.1
Activate AQ

Figure 16.10 Take 5 – record 16 bars of Brass 3.

- Using Groove: 2) 8th+8 record the 16 bars between the Locators .

• Save song – compare with project6/8.arr.

By selecting all the brass Parts we can examine the harmony. Three part, close voicing is used to provide a full brassy sound and for the first half of the tune the anacrusis is left to just Brass 1.

    The kick drum is providing the 'umph' required but a simple snare drum part will give it a lift.

Take 6

• Create a new MIDI Track (Ch 10) and rename it 'Snare Drum'.

> *Track Inspector*
> Output: LM-9
> Patchname: Beat Box
>
> *Status Bar*
> [Quantize 8]
>
> *Transport Bar*
> Locators: (L) 2.1.1 (R) 6.1.1
> Activate AQ

TIP

A s a rule of thumb, in three part sectional harmony, it's a good idea to have the outside parts form a duet and move together in parallel sixths where possible.

INFO

A nacrusis – posh word for 'pick-up' ! – the note(s) preceding the main part of a musical phrase.

• Using Groove: 2)8th+8 record the four bars between the Locators (Figure 16.11) and copy the resulting Part three more times to complete 16 bars.

Figure 16.11 Take 6 – record four bars of snare drum.

We need to dispense with the 'fill' duplicated in bar 11 (where the melody temporarily breaks the rhythmic pattern) so delete the Snare events at 11. 3. 3. 320 and 11. 4. 3. 320.

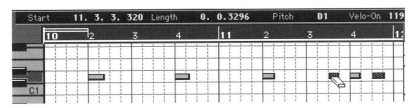

Figure 16.11a Delete the snare events.

• Save song – compare with project6/9.arr.

The entire 16 bars will stand a repeat, but first:

- With the Song Position Pointer on 2.1.1, use the Scissors Tool (left), make a cut between bars 1 and 2 on the Brass 1 Track , to isolate the 'pick-up'.
- Drag a copy of the new Part (bar 1) and drop it on top of bar 17 to create another pick-up (below left).
- With the Glue Tool, join all the Parts on each Track together between bars 2 – 18. Do not include the 'pick-up' at bar 1.
- Now set Locators at (L) 2.1.1 (R) 18.1.1 Select everything between [Edit>Select>Inside Locators] and repeat the Parts once [Structure>Repeat Parts>x1].

- Save song – compare with project6/10.arr.

The piece is now one minute long. Time for an ending. It has to be short and snappy to fit the brief. I have something in mind but I need to cut the duplicated pick-up (bar 33) on three Tracks.

- Select the brass 1 Track, and using the Key Editor delete all the notes between 33. 3 . 1 and 34. 1. 1.

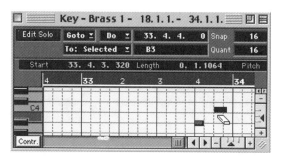

- Select the bass Track, and using the Key Editor delete all the notes between 33. 3 . 1 and 34. 1. 1.

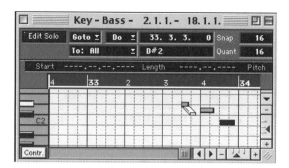

- Select the snare drum Track 6, and using the Drum or Key Editor, delete all the events between 33. 3 . 1 and 34. 1. 1.

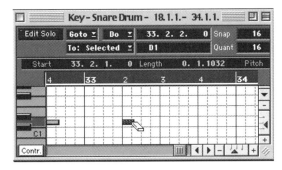

- Return to the brass 1 Track and using either Score or Key Editor, enter an eighth note, F4, at 33. 4. 1. Apply a velocity of 115 or so. It's the only note sounding here and needs to be strong.

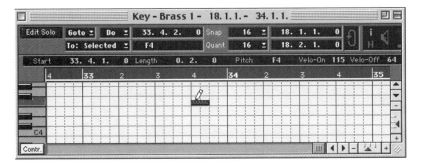

- Save song – compare with project6/11.arr.

Take 7

- Set the Locators to (L) 34. 1. 1 (R) 37. 1. 1
- Record the brass and kick drum parts in Figure 16.12.

Figure 16.12 Take 7 – record the brass and kick drum parts.

- Save song – compare with project6/12.arr.

The repeated section from bar 18 onwards sounds fine but there's room for something else. What will provide a lift? The whole piece is dominated by brass and a touch more will not do any harm. Something very high might do the trick. Maynard Ferguson style.

Take 8

• Create a new MIDI Track (Ch 5) and rename it 'Solo'.

Track Inspector
Output: USM
Program: 62
Patchname: Brass Section
Transpose 12

Status Bar
Quantize [8]

Transport Bar
Locators: (L) 18.1.1 (R) 37.1.1
Activate AQ

• Using Groove: 2)8th+8, record the solo brass part (Figure 16.13). Break it down into four bar chunks if need be. Note the transposition (12) in the Track Inspector. The notes in Figure 16.13 are written one octave lower than they sound.

Figure 16.13 Take 8 – record the solo brass part.

• Save song – compare with project6/13.arr.

Up to now we have left the harmony to the brass. On reflection, I think the piece may now benefit from some rhythm guitar. Something sparse and choppy.

Take 9

• Create a new MIDI Track (Ch 6) and rename it 'Guitar'.

Track Inspector
Output: USM
Program: 30
Patchname: Overdrive Guitar
Compression: 75%

Status Bar
Quantize [8]

Transport Bar
Locators: (L) 2.1.1 (R) 6.1.1
Activate AQ

Guitar parts are usually written an octave higher than they sound, even on a concert score. In this case, as we are playing a keyboard and giving a general impression of what a guitar might do here, it has been left at concert pitch. Play exactly as written.

• Using Groove: 2) 8th+8, record the four bar guitar Part between the Locators.

Figure 16.14 Take 9a – record the guitar; bars 2 – 6.

• Copy that Part to bar 6. We now have eight bars of guitar.
• Set Locators at (L)10.1.1 (R)14.1.1 and record Figure 16.15.

Figure 16.15 Take 9b – record the guitar; bars 10 – 14.

• Set Locators to (L)14.1.1 (R)18.1.1. and record Figure 16.16.

Figure 16.16 Take 9c – record the guitar; bars 14 – 18.

- Select the four guitar Parts between bars 2 and 18 and repeat them between bars 18 and 34 using Structure>Repeat Parts x1.
- Select just the last Part (30 – 34) and using the Key Editor delete the last two chords in the Part (33. 3. 3. 1280 and 33. 4. 3. 1280).

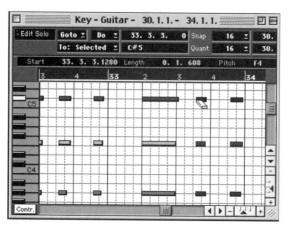

Then shorten the last remaining chord (33. 2. 1. 0) to an eighth note in length.

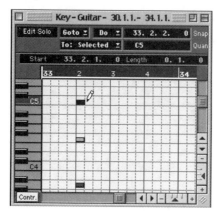

- Save song – compare with project6/14.arr.

Now for the coupe de grace!

Take 10

- Create a new MIDI Track (Ch 10) and rename it 'Referee' (Yes you've guessed it!).

Track Inspector
Output: USM
Program: 1
Patchname: Drums>Standard

Status Bar
Quantize [8]

Transport Bar
Locators: (L) 35.1.1 (R) 37.1.1
Activate AQ

• Using note B3 (Whistle) on the keyboard record Figure 16.17.

Figure 16.17 Take 10 – record the Referee!

• Save song – compare with project6/15.arr.

We add an audio Track

OK, apart from the mixing we're finished. Or are we? Now, I'm a saxophone player and although I'm happy enough with the solo brass part, I can mentally hear a tenor sax answering those brass phrases. So I recorded an Audio Track.

Obviously, every reader can't follow me step by step as with the MIDI side of things so far (unless they happen to play tenor sax) but I can explain the process. This will serve as a guide to the general principles involved in recording vocal tracks and acoustic instruments.

Before proceeding further, I would advise readers – if they have not yet done so – to read thoroughly their *Getting Started* booklet and *Getting into the Details* documents for a complete understanding of how Cubase VST handles the audio recording process. On the surface, in the Arrange window, Audio Parts look the same as MIDI Parts and are manipulated in a similar fashion. However, behind the scenes, in the Editors, things are very different.

Recording a saxophone is not so different to recording vocals. I used a good quality condenser mic, in preference to a dynamic type, and routed the signal through an external mixing console and then:

I created a new Track [Structure>Create Track] and changed it to an Audio Track by selecting the audio icon in the Track Class Column headed C. 'Master' appeared in the Output column.

Figure 16.18 I created an Audio Track named 'Tenor Sax'...

I selected Chn 1 in the channel column and renamed the Track 'Tenor Sax'.

... and renamed the Track.

TIP

*C*ubase saves audio files to disk using Track names. To make them easy to find, rename Audio Tracks before actually recording.

TIP

*E*asily overlooked – ensure that the tiny 'In' button is lit to enable metering of the input signal and maybe save hours of head scratching!

I selected 'Mono' (as opposed to Stereo) in the Track Inspector (see Figure 15.2). I selected the input in the Inspector by clicking on the right-hand side of the Input button and choosing IN 1 L from the pop-up menu. My audio signal was entering on the left input of my stereo card.

I activated the Input button by clicking on the left-hand side. It illuminated. I activated the Record Enable button. It illuminated.

I opened the VST Channel Mixer [Panel>VST Channnel Mixer] and checked that the Input button, at the top of the fader strip, was illuminated (Figure 15.3). This is a duplicate of the Input button on the Inspector. I activated the 'In' button above the level meter. It illuminated (Figure 15.4).

At this point I began playing the saxophone – partly to warm up, and partly to check my input level. I adjusted this by using the output fader on my external mixer until satisfactory levels were achieved in the VST Channel Mixer.

By blowing as loud as I knew I would be when actually recording, the red clipping indicator (just above the In button) was lighting up. I reduced the fader level on my external mixer until a satisfactory input level (around –3dB, for safety) was showing in the VST Channel Mixer. The Fader on the VST Channel Mixer is not used to alter the input level, only the recorded signal. To avoid distortion, make sure the input signal does not exceed 0.0dB.

Everybody finds their own way of doing things. It's possible to Cycle Record several takes and either choose the best or edit them. The document *Using Cycled Recording for a 'perfect' take* in the *Getting Into Details* manual supplied with Cubase VST 5 tells you how. I prefer to record a 'take' and listen back. If I like it, great. If I don't, I delete it and record another straight away. In Cubase this 'take' is not actually deleted but remains on the hard disk, in the Audio Pool, so I can change my mind and recall it later.

Playing the saxophone and recording – pressing record buttons on and off at the same time etc. – is an unwieldy, and potentially dangerous task to say the least. Fortunately the whole process can be automated in Cubase VST (not the sax playing of course!). Before recording the sax:

I muted the Solo Brass on Track 5, set the Locators at (L) 18. 1. 1 (R) 26. 1. 1 and activated both the Punch In and Punch Out buttons on the Transport Bar.

Figure 16.19 Punch In and Punch Out buttons.

I scrolled back a few bars and pressed Play. When the Song Pointer reached bar 18, on came the red light and Cubase was in record mode. I blasted away on the tenor sax for eight bars, and when bar 26 arrived, off went the red light, and back on the stand went the tenor sax. A brand new Audio Part looking very much like its MIDI counterpart had appeared on the Audio Track (Ch 1).

After listening back I decided that I could do better. I could have sliced it up and dropped in and out at various points but, in my experience it's better to get things down in one take. I deleted the Part (remember this is non-destructive, it's still in the Audio Pool) and repeated the recording process. This time I'm happy. I can live with that.

Again, I know what I want between bars 26 and 30, and I know it's not easy, which is why I didn't include it in the first take! A very high altissimo C (concert Bb) may well need a few attempts. It did. After a satisfactory take I moved on to the last four measures. Easy by compari-son. One take was all that was necessary. I now had three audio Parts. After playing the whole piece, I decided to keep them all.

I don't have unlimited hard disk space, (and neither, I expect, do you) so next: I opened the Audio Pool [Panels>Audio Pool]. Here I found all the unwanted takes – all neatly numbered tk 1, 2, 3 etc. – that I had deleted from the Arrange page earlier. I only want to keep the three good takes.

From the Audio Pool File menu (Figure 16.20) I selected Delete Unused Files and was confronted with a dialogue box warning me that this operation could not be undone. I was confident the files would not be needed here or in other songs and went ahead

Figure 16.20 Delete unused files in the Audio Pool. Use with care!.

The mix

I kept it simple and a summary is all that is necessary.

• MIDI Track Mixer Settings: (Figure 16.21).

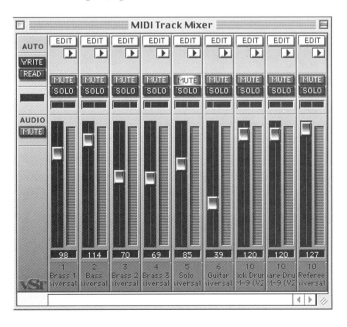

Figure 16.21 project6.all – MIDI Track Mixer settings.

- Bass and drums are in the centre.
- Brass 1 is in the centre because it carries the tune.
- Brass 2 and 3 are supporting parts and are set at lower levels than Brass 1. However they are panned left and right and provide the main stereo spread.
- Solo brass is in the centre but not too loud.
- Guitar is panned left and kept low in the mix.

USM output settings

Figure 16.22 project6.all – USM Output settings.

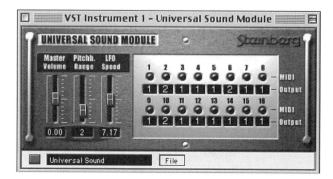

I wanted reverb on the brass and sax Tracks so MIDI Channels 2, 6 and 10 (bass, guitar and percussion – the referee!) were routed to Output 2. The remainder (brass) are free for effects treatment on Output 1.

Send Effects

Figure 16.23 (right) project6.all – reverb mix of 50%.

Figure 16.24 The Tenor Sax can be routed through Soft Clip.

- 'Reverb' with Long and Warm Preset.

VST Channel Settings

- FX – a small amount of reverb was applied to tenor sax (Chn 1) and brass (USM 1).
- DYN – In the Dynamics section, the tenor sax could be routed through Soft Clip which acts as an automatic limiter on the signal and provides a touch of warmth to the digital recording. Try it.

View and listen to the result in project6.all alternately muting Track 5 (MIDI – solo brass) and Track 10 (Audio – tenor sax) to compare versions.

Create illusions – a big band radio jingle

17

sTo examine the Cubase files for this chapter: from the CD, copy the folder named 'big band' to your computer.

Jack has a small studio set-up and runs Cubase VST. Some local jingle work has been coming his way recently and a client calls to say that he needs some big band swing music, 1940s style. He really liked the Vangelis 1980s style synth music Jack supplied for the last job, but this is a bit different. A jazz big band is comprised of 17 instruments for a start and some pretty smart arranging techniques are needed. He decides to take on the challenge, confident that he can handle the sequencing. A friend, fresh from music college, agrees to score the 30 seconds of music required.

A day or so later his mate arrives clutching a 'hot' score for five saxes, four trumpets, four trombones and rhythm section, but they soon realize that no matter how skilfully things are sequenced using sampled sounds, the end result will not be convincing enough.

It's always a little tricky to sequence acoustic instruments, even with the very best sampled instrument sounds available, but the problem seems to compound itself when a large ensemble is needed such as a symphony orchestra. Brass bands are particularly difficult, due mainly to the fact that all the instruments are using the same type of sample. As the layers are piled on, a kind of MIDI soup develops. The problem is not quite so bad with a jazz big band, but care must taken to avoid too thick a texture.

Back to Jack's problem. What's the solution? Well, he could book a large studio or a local hall and hire 17 musicians, but in Jack's case, that's the route to bankruptcy. He has another idea. Apart from being a dab hand at arranging his pal also plays a mean saxophone. Jack decides to create an illusion.

Audio and MIDI Tracks combined

Once a large collection of MIDI instruments are combined as an ensemble it soon becomes obvious, even to the untrained ear, that synthesized sounds are being used. In Jack's case hiring 17 musicians is out of the question so he decides to ask his friend to replace the virtual saxophone section with the real thing. Five saxes are used in the score, two altos, two tenors and one baritone. He doesn't own a baritone so they decide to leave that as it is.

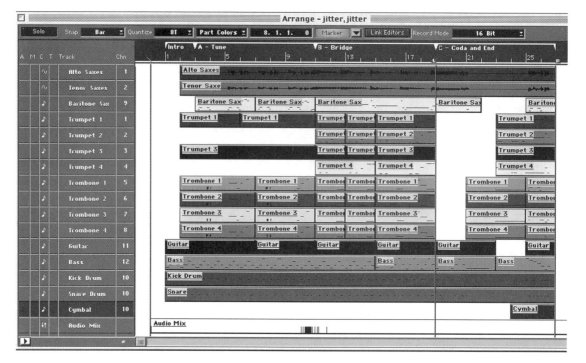

Figure 17.1 'Jitterbug Jump' –
Arrange window view.

- Open Cubase Song File bigband/jitter.all
- Set the MIDI Track Outputs to the Universal Sound Module.

Entitled 'Jitterbug Jump' this is a 29 second 'sting,' composed in a1940s big band swing style and originally intended for use as library music.

This version has in fact been heavily edited from around five minutes to 30 seconds to achieve a punchy fast moving sound track suitable for the role of background music to a radio jingle or similar use. This editing requires a great deal of savagery on the part of the composer. It's no good being precious about one's art in a commercial world. Things have to go. In this case it was four and a half minutes of music including a tenor saxophone jazz chorus. The Marker Track indicates the construction.

Intro	This was reduced from four bars to 2.
A	The main tune, carried by trumpets, backed by riffing saxes and wailing trombones and reduced from 16 bars to eight.
B	The bridge, eight bars long and carried by saxophones survives intact!
C	A huge cut to a coda and ending.

By moving quickly from one section to another within a 30 second framework the listener's attention is kept throughout. Of course it all gets shoved in the background behind somebody talking anyway, and that's another reason not get too intense about cutting things out.

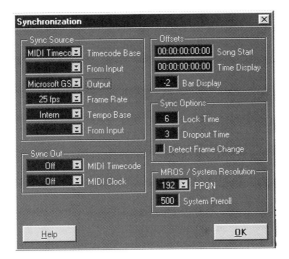

Figure 17.2 The Generate SMPTE feature.

From top to bottom we have two audio Tracks, 11 MIDI Tracks, three drum Tracks and a mixer Track.

The first Track contains two alto saxophones and the second two tenor saxophones. You may be wondering if I used two players on each Track. I did not. Neither did I play two saxophones at once! 'Jitterbug Jump' was originally recorded on a 16 track analogue tape machine and each saxophone had its own track. To save unnecessary overload on my computer CPU (and yours) I doubled them up whilst transferring them across to Cubase.

The original analogue recording had been striped with SMPTE time code from a source other than Cubase. To ensure the audio would be locked to the MIDI in Cubase after it was transferred, I re-striped the tape with SMPTE time code generated from within Cubase [Options>Generate SMPTE...].

SMPTE generated by Cubase is more reliable because it runs at the same speed as the audio hardware. A SMPTE to MTC (Midi Time Code) convertor was used to synchronize Cubase and the analogue tape machine. A new set of MIDI Tracks were sequenced afterwards to accompany the Audio Tracks.

It's worth taking a closer look at 'Jitterbug Jump' because many of the topics and principles discussed in this book so far are used here.

The saxophone section
Just as a magician distracts our attention away from what he does not wish us to see, the same technique is used here. By keeping the saxophone section fairly prominent (but never dominant) our attention is focused on these 'real' instruments rather than the artificial ones. Even the fifth member of the section – the sampled baritone sax – is not really noticeable as such. There is a fair bit of unison doubling throughout and had this been a MIDI saxophone section, much pruning would have be needed to 'thin' the texture at those points. With real saxes it doesn't matter. The more the merrier.

The trumpet section

Only the lead trumpet has been assigned to the USM preset 'Trumpet' (Prg. 57) This sets it apart from trumpets 2, 3 and 4 which use the 'Brass Section' preset (Prg. 62) Where unison doubling occurs, care has been taken to avoid using the same USM voice. For example, in the opening bars, only trumpet 1 and 3 are playing. If trumpets 2 and 4 were added, MIDI soup would result. However, if this were a real brass trumpet section all four trumpets would be playing in unison here.

The trombone section

Trombones 1 and 2 have been assigned to the USM preset 'Trombone' (Prg. 58) and trombones 3 and 4 to the 'Brass Section' preset (Prg. 62). As with the trumpets, although unison doubling does occur it only happens on separate presets to avoid unnecessary thickening of the texture.

Pitch bend was used between measures 2 and 11 to create the semitone slurs. Viewed In the Score Editor, the notes are displayed at a constant pitch. Use either the Key, List or Controller Editors to view the Pitch Bend data.

The rhythm section

Piano has been omitted. In a real big band it would very likely be used. However the acoustic guitar provides all the rhythm and harmony needed here along with acoustic bass. Guitar chord voicing is mostly open and restricted, in the main, to four notes.

The drums have been split over three Tracks. In this kind of music a real drummer may well play his snare drum on all four beats in a bar and accent the second and fourth. However we achieve much the same effect here by omitting the first and third beats.

The mix

The mix Track contains some automation data where the saxes are increased in volume around bar 10. Apart from that, Volume and Pan data were created using the MIDI Track Mixer. The instruments are panned roughly as a big-band would be seated. The only exception being bass and drums which are placed in the centre for balance. A small amount of reverb has been added to the saxophones. Any more would have created too much of a distancing effect.

75% compression was added to all the MIDI Tracks as they were played and smooths out any jerkiness due to my keyboard playing shortcomings!

Project 7 – a TV sitcom theme

18

Musical objective
- To construct a melody using only the notes of a blues scale.
- Fill in the harmonic and rhythmic background with the sounds of a blues band.

New Cubase skills
- Use Compress and Limit in the Dynamics processor.

Preparation
- Create a folder called 'mywork7' or something similar in which to save your work.
- Open a New Arrangement [File>New Arrangement].
- On the Transport Bar, set the Time Signature to 4/4.
- Our tempo for this piece is 105 bpm. Set this in the Mastertrack.
- In the 'mywork7' folder, save as Song File myproj7.all or something similar.
- From the CD, copy the folder named 'project7' to your computer.

The brief
You've been commissioned to write a theme tune for a television sitcom. The main characters are two young, likeable 'no-hopers'. You know the kind of thing. They can't pull the girls, they can't keep their jobs, and at the end of every episode, despite temporary success, are back where they started. The music required is to be fairly upbeat (it is a comedy) but at the same time, bluesy. Length: just under one minute. The producer is keen on tenor sax and if possible, would like it featured.

This is a bit of a tough one. How do we keep it lively and at the same time bluesy? An upbeat 12 bar blues maybe. The problem with '12 bars' is that it is hard to find a distinctive melody to fit the rather played out chord sequence. In my experience it is always a good idea to work on the melody first and harmony second. So how do we compose an instrumental blues melody line? Well the blues scale is a good starting point.

When stuck for ideas whilst writing melodies it sometimes helps to limit oneself to just a few notes. A pentatonic scale for example will provide a set of notes suitable for something rustic and folky. In our case the blues scale, which contains one more note than a pentatonic scale, is just the job. A pentatonic tune in the key of C will consist of the notes C D E G A.

INFO

A pentatonic scale consists of just five notes and is found in a huge amount of folk music around the world as far ranging as China, Africa and Scotland. Auld Lang Syne, for example, uses only the notes of the pentatonic scale.

133

TIP

It's possible to invent simple tunes very quickly using the pentatonic scale on the piano. How? – by using only the black notes starting with F#.

OK, which key? Well tenor sax was mentioned in the brief. The key of Bb/Gm is a good key for tenor and actually puts the player in the nice easy key of C/Am. So the blues scale for this key is G Bb C C# D F G. 'That's all very well,' I can hear you say, 'the blues scale is fine for improvisation but surely it is too limiting for composing a theme tune.' Well, it's surprising just how much can be done with those six notes particularly if more than one blues scale is used. For this tune we are also going to use the C blues scale, C Eb F F# G Bb C and the D blues scale, D F G G# A C D.

A blues scale has only one more note than the pentatonic scale, but what a difference it makes! It's used frequently by jazz and rock soloists alike. In the key of C it will consist of: C D Eb E G A. but is usually played beginning on A, like this: A C D Eb E G A and referred to as the A blues scale.

Why does the key of Bb put the tenor saxophone player in the key of C? Because it is a transposing instrument. A tenor saxophone is pitched in Bb. When a pianist plays the note Bb, at concert pitch, the tenor sax player blows a tone higher – the note C. Likewise if the pianist was to play Eb then the tenor sax player would again play a tone higher – the note F. Of course they are really both playing the same note. The tenor sax player is just thinking, and as far as he is concerned, playing in a different key.

So, music for the tenor saxophone is notated a tone higher than it actually sounds. Now this is sometimes convienient for the player and reduces the number of flats he would have to play if his instrument was pitched in C. The key of Ab, concert pitch, (four flats) puts him in Bb (two flats) for instance. However, it is not so good for him in sharp keys. For example, the key of C, concert pitch, will put him in the key of D containing two sharps. The key of E (four sharps) puts him in F# (six sharps).

Other common transposing instruments are:

Bb   trumpet, clarinet, soprano sax
Eb   alto sax, baritone sax
F   cor anglais, french horn

Some instruments, such as the piccolo and guitar, sound one octave higher than they are notated on the staff. Others such as the double bass and bass guitar sound one octave lower than written.

To gain an overall picture, at this point you may prefer to listen to the finished thing rather than just let things unfold. To do so, load project7/project7.all

You will need to set the Output columns to the VST Instruments called Universal Sound Module and LM-9 otherwise you may not hear anything! See the Appendix – Page 194 – for details.

Take 1

• Create a MIDI Track (Ch 1)) and rename it 'Piano'.

Because a blues shuffle feel is required here the Quantization has been set to 8T.

The melody will eventually be played on tenor sax but we will construct it first using a piano pre-set.

- Record the melody in Figure 18.1. How you do it is up to you. If you are an accomplished keyboard player it can be done in one pass. It's more likely that you will opt to record it in sections (Figure 18.2). To help you decide how to break it down here's a brief analysis of the melody.

Figure 18.1 Take 1 – record the melody.

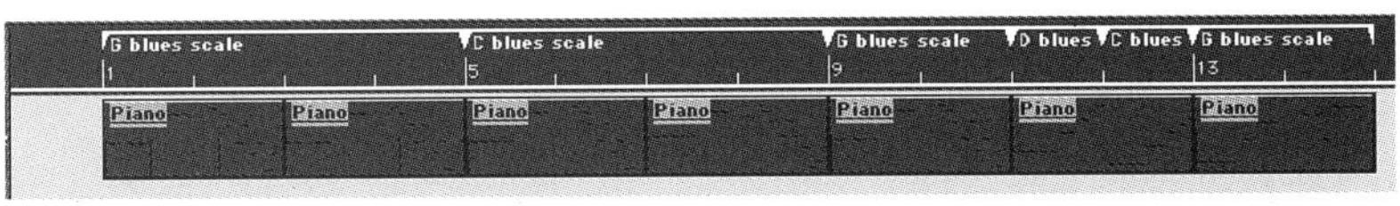

Figure 18.2 The melody can be recorded in sections.

Bar 1 poses a musical question, bar 2 answers it. Bars 1 to 3 then, are a phrase and use all six notes of the G blues scale. The phrase is repeated between bars 3 and 5 but – for variation and continuation – the last note has been changed from Bb to G. Bars 5 to 7 are a repetition of the first phrase but this time use the C blues scale. They are repeated between bars 7 and 9 with pitch variation on the last two beats. Bars 9 to 11 are an exact repetition of the first phrase using the G blues scale.

Bar 11 uses the D blues scale. Bar 12 is a repetition but uses the C blues scale. Bar 13 is an exact repetition of bar 1. Bar 14 is a new ending phrase using part of the G blues scale.

- Save song – compare with project7/1.arr.

When loading *my* Cubase Arrange files into *your* Song file version for comparison, remember to:

1 Check that the Universal Sound Module and any other VST Instruments needed have been loaded.
2 Ensure the Output columns display the USM and any other VST Instruments needed.
3 To avoid confusion, close down *my* Arrange file version before any further saving of *your* Song file.

That's a chunk of the tune finished. The backing suggests itself.

Take 2

- Create another MIDI Track (Ch 2) and rename it 'Bass'.

Track Inspector
Output: USM
Program 34
Patchname: Electric Bass (finger)
Transp –12

Status Bar
Quantize [8T]

Transport Bar
Activate AQ

For the bass a nice simple eighth note shuffle on the root note of each blues scale is really all that's needed. You can of course improvise on this, as would a real player. Keeping it simple though, for now at least, will help establish a clear harmonic structure.

- Record Take 2 (Figure 18.3). Even though the eighth notes are written straight, play them with a triplet feel. Again how you break it down is up to you. It is not too difficult to play in one pass, except maybe for the last bar, which can be done separately. Have a go!

- Save song – compare with project7/2.arr.

Figure 18.3 Take 2 – record the electric bass.

Take 3

• Create another 3 MIDI Tracks (Ch 10) and rename them 'Kick Drum' 'Snare Drum' and 'Crash Cym'.

Track Inspector
Output: LM-9
Patchname: Acoustic

Status Bar
Quantize [8T]

Transport Bar
Activate AQ

Ensure that the General MIDI Drum Map has been loaded [File>Open from Library>General MIDI Drum Map]
    Again simplicity is the key to a solid track here so:

• Set the Locators to (L) 1. 1. 1 (R) 14. 1 1 and on the kick drum Track record Take 3a – Figure 18.4 (C1).

Figure 18.4 Take 3a – record the kick drum.

- Record a back beat snare (D1) on the snare drum Track (Figure 18.5).

Figure 18.5 Take 3b – record the snare drum.

- Set the Locators to (L) 14. 1. 1 (R) 15. 1. 1 and record the snare fill (Figure 18.6).

Figure 18.6 Take 3c – record the snare drum fill.

- On the Crash Cym Track record a crash (C#2) on the first beat of bars 1, 5, and 9.

- Save song – compare with project7/3.arr.

It's coming along isn't it? Play it through and try to imagine the two characters, maybe in a dole queue or being rebuffed by two pretty girls. What next? Well we have the basics of a blues band. Why not add guitar and organ to complete the line up.

Take 4

- Create another MIDI Track (Ch 3) and rename it 'Guitar'.

Track Inspector
Output: USM
Program 31
Patchname: Distortion Guitar
Comp: 50%

Status Bar
Quantize [8T]

Transport Bar
Activate AQ

Guitar parts are usually written an octave higher than they sound, even on a concert score. In this case, as we are playing a keyboard, it has been left at concert pitch. Play exactly as written.

- Record Take 4 (Figure 18.7) on the guitar Track. You may well have to break it down into sections. Again it's a simple shuffle. A real guitar player would undoubtedly do more. However this creates the mood perfectly well.

- Save song – compare with project7/4.arr.

Figure 18.7 Take 4 – record the distortion guitar.

Take 5

- Create another MIDI Track (Ch 4) and rename it 'Organ'.

Track Inspector
Output: USM
Program 19
Patchname: Rock Organ
Comp: 50%

Status Bar
Quantize [8T]

Transport Bar
Activate AQ

To repeat the shuffle pattern again would be too much of a good thing. So what to play? Something a little more spaced out is called for that does not interfere with the melody. How about this:

- On the organ Track record Take 5 (Figure 18.8). Again, do it in sections if your keyboard skills are not too hot!

Figure 18.8 Take 5 – record the rock organ..

- Save song – compare with project7/5.arr.

Nothing more is needed except for the tenor sax, to replace the piano. Nothing more in the way of instruments that is. We only have about 30 seconds of music and the brief requires around one minute's worth. How do we extend it? Well, we could repeat it again. It might work but boredom would almost certainly creep in. No, something new is needed.

Think back to the brief. It's a comedy, but there's something a little sad about those characters. A slight change of mood could be established. But how do we do that without losing the feel? Continue to use the blues scale of course, to provide unity. Back to the piano Track and melody crafting.

Take 6

- Return to the piano Track (Ch 1) and set the Locators to (L) 15. 1. 1 (R) 17. 1. 1 and record Take 6a (Figure 18.9).

Figure 18.9 Take 6a – record the melody; bars 15 – 17.

This phrase uses the notes of the D blues scale and takes us up and away from what came before. We don't want to go higher so let's just repeat it in a descending pattern.

- Repeat the Part [Structure>Repeat Parts...] twice as far as measure 21.

We now have three Parts containing the same phrase.

- Select the second Part and transpose it down a tone (–2) [Functions>MIDI Functions/Transpose] to use a C blues scale.
- Select the third Part and transpose it down a fifth (–7) to use a G blues scale.
- Set the Locators to (L) 21. 1. 1 (R) 23. 1. 1 and record Take 6b (Figure 18.10).

Figure 18.10 Take 6b – record the melody; bars 21 – 23.

This takes us nicely back home to G, so:

- Set the Locators to (L) 23. 1. 1 (R) 25. 1. 1 and record Take 6c (Figure 18.11) to finish off at about 55 seconds. Luv'ly job!

Figure 18.11 Take 6c – record the melody; bars 23 – 25.

- Save song – compare with project7/6.arr.

Take 7

- Return to the bass Track (Ch 2).

In order to change the mood:

- Set the Locators to (L) 15. 1. 1 (R) 23. 1. 1 and record Figure 18.12. Do it in sections if you prefer.

Figure 18.12 Take 7a – record the electric bass; bars 15 – 23.

Set the Locators to (L) 23. 1. 1 (R) 25. 1. 1 and record the ending.
(Figure 18.13).

Figure 18.13 Take 7b – record
the electric bass; bars 23 –
25.

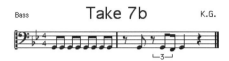

• Save song – compare with project7/7.arr.

Take 8

• Return to the organ Track (Ch 4).
• Set the Locators to (L) 15. 1. 1 (R) 23. 1. 1 and record Figure

Figure 18.14 Take 8a – record
the rock organ; bars 15 – 23.

18.14 (in sections if you prefer).
• Set the Locators to (L) 23. 1. 1 (R) 25. 1. 1 and record the ending.
(Figure 18.15)

Figure 18.15 Take 8 – record
the rock organ; bars 23 – 25.

• Save song – compare with project7/8.arr.

Take 9

• Return to the guitar Track (Ch 3)

How do we fit the distorted guitar into this more melancholic section?
The most obvious answer is to leave it out. Not only would it spoil the
mood, omitting it creates a nice sense of emptiness. However it will
boost the unison line in bar 22, so:

• Set the Locators to (L) 22. 1. 1 (R) 25. 1. 1 and record the ending
(Figure 18.16).

- Save song – compare with project 7/9.arr.

Figure 18.16 Take 9 – record the distortion guitar; bars 22 – 25.

Take 10

- Return to the kick drum Track (Ch 10).
- Set the Locators to (L) 23. 1. 1 (R) 25. 1. 1 and record the ending (Figure 18.17).

Figure 18.17 Take 10a – record the kick drum; bars 23 – 25.

- Return to the snare drum Track (Ch 10).
- Set the Locators to (L) 22. 1. 1 (R) 25. 1. 1 and record the ending (Figure 18.18).

Figure 18.18 Take 10b – record the snare drum; bars 22 – 25.

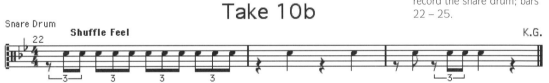

- Save song – compare with project 7/10.arr.

That's it. We're done. All that's needed is the tenor sax.

The mix

Open project7.all to hear and view the tenor sax Track which replaces the piano melody.

The tenor sax was recorded in one take using an external mixer and a Microtech Geffel condenser microphone. EQ was not used. After recording, the signal was treated with Reverb (VST Send Effect). The 'Vocal Plate' pre-set was used and the reverb signal reduced to 45% (Figure 18.19).

Figure 18.19 proj7mix.all – A reverb mix of 45% was used on the tenor sax.

Volume and Pan settings were made in the MIDI Track Mixer (Figure 18.20).

Figure 18.20 proj7mix.all – MIDI Track Mixer settings.

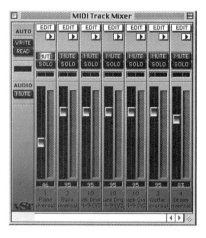

In order to apply a little reverb to the Guitar, channel 3 was routed to MIDI Output 2 in the Universal Sound Module editor. The remaining MIDI instruments are left on MIDI Output 1.

Play the piece through and you will notice that the tenor sax is exceeding 0.00dB in the Channel Mixer and the red clipping indicator illuminates as a warning (far left). The overload is around 3dB

Pulling the Channel Fader down helps, but of course reduces the entire signal and therefore the overall volume of what after all is the main instrument here. You can solve this problem by shaving the signal with the Limiter included with the VST Dynamics.

- Click on the button marked DYN near the top of the Channel Strip to open the Dynamics section (left).
- Activate the Limit button and set the threshold to around –5.00dB and activate the Auto Release button.

Setting the threshold. Limit is used to shave output signals above a set Threshold no matter how loud the input. In our case the output signal is peaking just above 3dB in a few places. A threshold of –5dB will do the trick.

- Return to the Channel Mixer and reset the red clipping indicator (Click on the red light to turn it off).

- Play the piece through and the problem should be solved. A nice loud signal with the dangerous peak levels reduced.

There is another way to tackle the problem:

Compression

- Turn Limit off.
- Activate the Compress button. It illuminates.
- Set a Threshold level of –27.0dB. This is the level at which Compress 'kicks in'. The audio signal above –27.0dB will be affected but nothing below.
- Set the Ratio to 3.5:1. This is the gain reduction applied to the signal above our Threshold level. For every 3.5dB the input level increases, the output level will increase only by one dB.
- Set the Attack at its lowest level, 0.1ms (virtually off). It's the initial bursts of sound at the beginning of the saxophone phrases that are causing the peaks and this setting will catch and compress them. Increasing this setting will let the initial attack through and the clipping will persist. Try it and see!
- Set the Release to Automatic.

Have a look at the Gain Reduction Meter whilst playing the piece through. It should show a reduction of about 10dB. So:

- Set the Make Up Gain level to 10.dB to compensate for the reduction.

All in all this is probably a more satisfactory solution than just applying Limit. Solo the Tenor Sax Track and you will notice an increase in noise. However, it's not unpleasant, rather more breathy in fact. Un-solo the Track and you'll notice that the sax is more focused in the mix.

19 Minimalism

To examine the Cubase files for this chapter: from the CD, copy the folder named 'minimal' to your computer.

Influence of minimalism in the media

Minimalism, as a musical art movement began in the early 1960s and was brought to prominence by Terry Riley with his enormously influential piece entitled 'In C'. It has been growing steadily ever since and composers such as Philip Glass, Steve Reich, John Adams, and Michael Nieman, are all very successful in this genre, writing music for film and theatre as well as concert works. Indeed the music of Glass and Reich is now so frequently imitated that the style can be heard on all manner of television commercials and incidental music.

Minimalist techniques

The cyclic and repetitive techniques used in minimalism often produce music of a static nature ideally suited for use with the moving image in the form of atmospheric soundtracks. These same techniques also make it ideal music for composing within sequencers such as Cubase. However because the music is essentially repetitive, many people mistakenly believe that all they have to do is compose a few measures and apply the Create Repeat function. This inevitably leads to very boring music indeed. To make it interesting, just as in all other forms of music, repetition must be combined with variation.

There are many techniques used in minimalism and the repetitive nature of the music often belies it's complexity. I have chosen two techniques used by minimalist composers for us to examine.

- Load minimal.all.
- Set the Output columns to Universal Sound Module.

This Song file contains two Arrangements. In minimal.all/minimal1.arr a gradual cumulative process of adding notes is used (Figures 19.1 and 19.2). It's a simple technique which quickly leads to very complex structures. Bar 1 contains a group of seven notes of equal length (eighth notes) which are repeated three times in succession. In bar 5 an extra note is added to the group and another at bar 9. If these 12 bars are cycled round we hear first an expanding effect and then as the cycle begins again a contracting one. The general melodic structure remains the same whilst quite different rhythmic structures emerge.

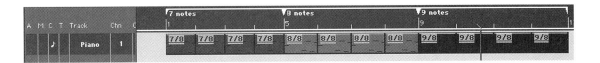

minimal1.arr

Repeating two or more rhythmic patterns of different lengths simultaneously is another technique. In minimal.all/minimal2.arr (Figures 19.3 and 19.4 the first right hand piano Part is two bars long and is repeated twice making a total of six measures. The left hand Part however is only one and a half bars long and has to be repeated three times to finish along with the right hand Part. When both Parts are viewed together in the Score Editor we see seven bars of music in 4/4. The result is rather hypnotic and although the music is repetitive no two measures are the same.

Figure 19.1 (top) minimal1.arr – Arrange window with Marker Track.

Figure 19.2 (lower) shows how a simple additive process quickly leads to a complex structure.

Figure 19.3 minimal2.arr – two repeating patterns of different lengths playing simultaneously …

Figure 19.4 …the result is rather hypnotic.

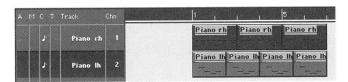

minimal2.arr

In the next chapter we will use similar techniques to those above and combine them with pre-recorded audio parts to produce a minimalist piece of music.

Project 8 – a minimalist soundtrack 20

Musical objectives
- Use a pentatonic scale to construct a simple ostinato, oriental in character and suitable for manipulation in a minimalist fashion.
- Decide upon instrumentation to create an atmosphere for film clip depicting an oriental landscape.
- Create 'cycles' using repetitive techniques to generate new patterns.
- Introduce new musical elements that coincide with, and enhance the addition of a procession in the landscape film.

New Cubase skills
- Set Pitch Bend Range in the USM.
- Further use of compression in the Dynamics section of the VST Channel Settings.
- Further use of the limiter in the Dynamics section of the VST Channel Settings.
- Create a 'fade out' with Mix Automation.

Preparation
- From the CD, copy the folder named 'project8' to your computer.
- On your computer, create a folder called 'mywork8' or something similar in which to save your work.
- Open a New Arrangement [File>New Arrangement].
- On the Transport Bar, set the Time Signature to 4/4.
- Our tempo for this piece is 108 bpm. Set this in the Mastertrack.
- In the 'mywork8' folder, save as Song File myproj8.all or something similar.

The brief
Using minimalist techniques, compose a piece of music about one and a half minutes long for use as a soundtrack with an oriental landscape scene. The scene first opens with an empty landscape. After about 20 seconds we see the beginnings of a procession of people appear on the horizon. The procession winds its way into the foreground. After about 55 seconds we can see that the procession contains not only marching figures but acrobats and elephants. After about 1 minute and 30 seconds the procession has passed and gradually disappears from view.

As with previous projects, you may prefer to listen to the finished article before going further. To do this, open project8/project8.all and play it through a few times.

You will need to set the MIDI Track Output columns to the VST Instrument called Universal Sound Module otherwise you may not hear anything!

Take 1

• Create a Stereo Audio Track (Ch 1+2) and rename it 'Guitar'.

Track Inspector
Stereo

Transport Bar
Locators: (L) 1.1.1 (R) 3.1.1

guitar.PRT

Figure 20.1 Parts can be saved too. They have a .prt extension.

• Ensure that Locators are at the correct position and from the project8 folder open guitar.prt (Figure 20.1). This is a pre-recorded audio Part containing a very simple ostinato which is repeated throughout this composition. It actually consists of an acoustic guitar and a harp sample.
• Repeat the Part (bars 1 – 3) six times as far as bar 15 (Figure 20.2a).

Figure 20.2a Repeat the Part six times

Have a look at the Track in the Audio Editor [Edit>Edit]. Note how each audio Part is displayed on a separate 'lane' (Figure 20.2b).

Figure 20.2b Each Audio Part is displayed on a separate lane.

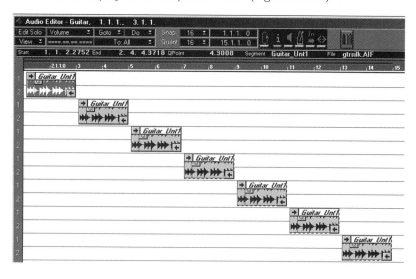

INFO

*A*n audio Part includes references to the audio file events. The audio files are imported into the Arrangement or Song, without having to import them separately in the pool.

We are going to do a rough mix as we go on this one so:

- Open the VST Channnel Mixer and set the Channel Fader to around −10 db (about the halfway mark) and pan the stereo signal hard left and right (Figure 20.3).

- Save song – compare with project8/1.arr.

When loading *my* Cubase Arrange files into *your* Song file version for comparison, remember to:

1 Check that the Universal Sound Module and any other VST Instruments needed have been loaded.
2 Ensure the Output columns display the USM and any other VST Instruments needed.
3 To avoid confusion, close down *my* Arrange file version before any further saving of *your* Song file.

Figure 20.3 Set the fader at the halfway mark and pan the stereo hard left and right.

Take 2

- Create a MIDI Track (Ch 1) and rename 'Pizzicato Str.'

Track Inspector
Output: USM
Program: 46
Patchname: Pizzicato Strings

Status Bar
Quantize [8]

Transport Bar
Locators: (L) 3.1.1 (R) 5.1.1
Activate AQ

The brief requires something oriental in character and the most obvious thing that comes to mind is the pentatonic scale E G A B D. However the guitar is only playing two notes and it would be nice to keep things simple. So let's drop the G and A. That leaves E B and D with which to build another ostinato. A light texture is required. How about pizzicato strings? Violins are not oriental instruments as such, but when plucked strings are used they provide that kind of flavour.

- Record the ostinato in Figure 20.4 and Quantize to value 8.

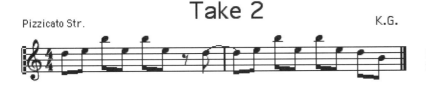

Take 2

Pizzicato Str.   K.G.

Figure 20.4 Take 2 – record the pizzicato string ostinato.

Minimalism, as we know, is about repetition. We also know that variation is needed to stimulate interest so we are now going to duplicate the Part just recorded and then work on each resulting Part individually.

- Repeat the pizzicato string Part (bars 3 – 5) five times as far as bar 15. Now here's what we are going to do. Each Part will keep its rhythmic structure but the notes will be changed according to a simple rule:

- The first Part (bars 1 – 3) remains unaltered. We'll refer to this as the 'original Part'
- The second Part (bars 3 – 5) begins on the second note of the original Part
- The third Part (bars 5 – 7) begins on the third note of the original Part

Figure 20.5 The 'original Part' is transformed into a 12 bar ostinato.

- The process is repeated on the remaining Parts until we have a 12 bar ostinato named 'Cycle 1' in the Marker Track (Figure 20.5).

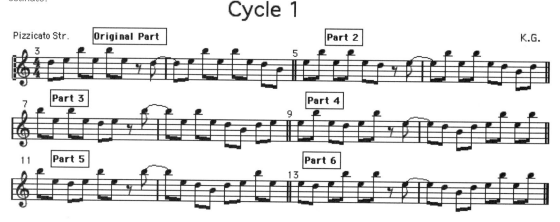

- Save song – compare with project8/2.arr.

Take 3

- Create another MIDI Track (Ch 2) and rename it 'Viola'.

Track Inspector
Output: USM
Program: 42
Patchname: Viola

Status Bar
Snap [1/2]
Quantize [8]

- Return to the pizzicato Track and glue the pizzicato string Parts together as one.
- Ensure Snap has been changed to [1/2] and drag a copy of the pizzicato string Part to 4. 3. 1 on the viola Track (Figure 20.6).
- Rename the Part 'Viola' and play back the piece. The 12 bar ostinato 'Cycle 1' begins with the pizzicato strings and is echoed as a canon, 1 1/2 bars later by the viola. Things are becoming interesting even though only three notes have so far been used. Already we have the oriental backdrop required.

Figure 20.6 'Cycle 1' begins with pizzicato strings and is echoed as a canon by the Viola.

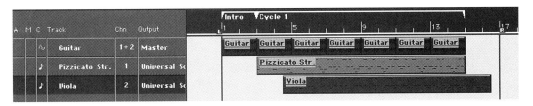

- Open the MIDI Track Mixer and, depending on how you played, adjust the volume levels of the pizzicato strings and the viola. Because they are both playing essentially the same thing, and to avoid confusion, pan the viola to the right and pizzicato strings to the left.

- Save song – compare with project8/3.arr.

Take 4

- Create a mono audio Track (Ch 3) and rename it 'Oboe'.

Track Inspector
Mono
IN 1L

Transport Bar
Locators: (L) 3.1.1 (R) 7.1.1

INFO

A canon contains musical imitation. A melodic strand is repeated after a certain interval, in our case after one and a half bars. There are many forms of canon. The imitation may be at the octave, or another interval such as a fifth. Simple canons take the form of a round such as London's Burning or Frere Jacques.

- Ensure that the Locators are at the correct position and from the project8 folder open oboe.prt, a pre-recorded audio Part which contains a four bar ostinato melody.
- Repeat the Part (bars 3 – 7) twice, as far as bar 15.
- Open the VST Channel Mixer and set the volume to around –7db for the Oboe

- Save song – compare with project8/4.arr.

- Select the guitar, pizzicato str. and oboe Parts between (L) 3. 1. 1 (R) 15. 1. 1 (Cycle 1) and repeat them three times as far as bar 51.

- Select the viola Parts between (L) 4. 3. 1 (R) 16. 3. 1 and repeat them three times as far as 52. 3. 1.

- Save song – compare with project8/4a.arr.

We have reached the point where the beginning of a procession appears.

Take 5

- Create a MIDI Track (Ch 3) and rename it 'Strings 1'.

Track Inspector
Output: USM
Program: 49
Patchname: SynthStrings1

Status Bar
Quantize 8
Snap [Bar]

Transport Bar
Locators: (L) 11.1.1 (R) 17.1.1

- Ensure that Snap has been returned to [Bar] on the Status Bar.
- Record the strings (Figure 20.7) between the Locators. To achieve the descending glissando from D down to G just play the note D2 and use the pitch bend controller on your MIDI keyboard for the slide down.

Figure 20.7 Take 5 – record the SynthStrings.

Figure 20.8 USM Pitch Bend range set to 7.

This is easy if you set the Universal Sound Module's Pitch Bend range to 7 (Figure 20.8). You can then slide all the way down and land safely on the G below.

Another way to do it is to record the note first and add the glissando afterwards in the Controller Editor [Edit>Controller] (Figure 20.9). This can be drawn with the Pencil Tool. However, in my experience it is usually best to record it as you play. Less of a fiddle!

It's also worth checking to see that Pitch Bend has been reset at the end of the note. If not the next note on that channel will sound terribly wrong! Do this in the List Editor. (Figure 20.10)

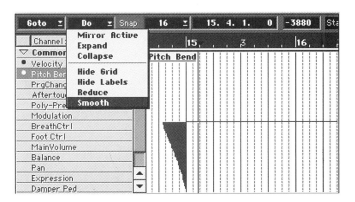

Figure 20.9 You can also draw the glissando in the Controller Edit window.

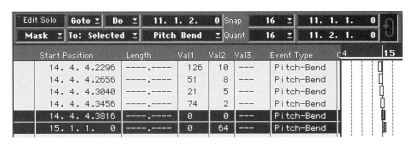

Figure 20.10 Check that Pitch Bend has been re-set in the List Editor (Val1=0, Val2=64).

- Create another MIDI Track (Ch 4) and rename it 'Strings 2'.
- Copy the Strings 1 Part to the new Track (Ch 4) at the same Locator positions and in the Track Inspector transpose the Track (not the Part) down an octave (−12). It will help identification if you rename the new Part 'Strings 2.'
- In the MIDI Track Mixer adjust the volume for Strings 1 and 2. Avoid having them too loud. I panned them hard left and right for separation. The effect is more dramatic too.

- Save song – compare with project8/5.arr.

> ## INFO
>
> *Warning – set the pitch bend range for the USM to 7 (Figure 20.8) otherwise you will not hear the glissando contained in project8/5.arr.*

Take 5a

- Return to the Strings 1 Track (Ch 3) and set the Locators at (L) 17.1.1 (R) 23.1.1 and record a second glissando in the same manner as the first (Figure 20.11). Again, copy the resulting Part to the Strings 2 Track (Ch 4) and rename it. It will play back one octave lower if transposition of the Track has been set correctly.

Figure 20.11 Take 5a – record a second glissando.

We have now created a sense of expectancy. Something just has to happen after this.

- Save song – compare with project8/5a.arr.

We have now reached the point where the full procession including the acrobats and animals is in view.

Take 6

- Return to the String 1 Track.
- Set Locators at (L) 27. 1. 1 (R) 31. 1. 1 and record the strings (Figure 20.12).

Figure 20.12 Take 6 – record the SynthStrings 1; bars 27 – 31.

- Copy the resulting Part to the String 2 Track and rename it. Check that it sounds an octave lower.
- Select both the String 1 and 2 Parts between bars 27 – 32 and Repeat them three times as far as bar 43.

- Save song – compare with project8/6.arr.

Take 6a

- Return to the String 1 Track.
- Set Locators at (L) 43. 1. 1 (R) 53. 1. 1 and record the strings in Figure 20.13.

Figure 20.13 Take 6a – record the SynthStrings 1; bars 43 – 53.

- Copy the resulting Part to the String 2 Track and rename it. Check that it sounds an octave lower.
- Save song – compare with project8/6a.arr.

We now have strings, one octave apart, playing a moving line and creating a contrast with the repeating ostinatos above. Something more is needed to add extra weight, and bass and drums are the obvious choice. However I think a slap bass is needed to give the edge needed to cut through those low strings.

Take 7

- Create another mono audio Track (Ch 4) and rename it 'Bass Guitar.'

Track Inspector
Mono
IN 1R

Transport Bar
Locators: (L) 27.1.1 (R) 31.1.1

- Ensure that the Locators are at the correct position and from the project8 folder open bass.prt This is a four bar riff derived from the ostinatos playing above it but also follows the harmonic progression of the string line.
- Repeat the Part three times as far as bar 43.
- Set the Locators at (L) 43. 1. 1 (R) 45. 1. 1 and from your mywork8 folder open bass2.prt to complete the bass line. This will more than likely open on a separate, newly created Track. Simply move the new Part to its correct location (bar 43, bass Track, Ch 4) and delete the unwanted Track afterwards.

- Save song – compare with project8/7.arr.

- In the VST Channel Mixer leave the volume at 0.00 db

All that's needed are the drums.

Take 8

- Create a MIDI Track (Ch 10) and rename it 'Drums'.

Track Inspector
Output: USM
Patchname: Standard

Status Bar
Snap [Bar]
Quantize [8]

Transport Bar
Locators: (L) 26. 1. 1 (R) 44. 1. 1

- Ensure that the General MIDI Drum map has been loaded [File>Open from Library>General MIDI Drum Map].

- Record the drum Part. Bar 26 is an intro fill. 27 to 43 is a two bar pattern repeated using Bass Drum 1 (C1) and Electric Snare (E1) Bar 43 is a Cymbal Crash (C#2) (Figure 20.14). It can all be played quite easily in one pass on a keyboard but break it down if need be. I used Iterative Quantization to tighten things a little.
- Adjust the volume in the MIDI Track Mixer.

Figure 20.14 Take 8 – record the Drum part.

- Save song – compare with project8/8.arr.

Take 9

- Create another MIDI Track – (Ch 10) and rename it 'Tambourine'.

Track Inspector
Output: USM
Patchname: Standard

Status Bar
Snap [Bar]
Quantize [8]

Transport Bar
Locators: (L) 27. 1. 1 (R) 43. 1. 1

- The tambourine (F#2) plays a one bar pattern (Figure 20.15) repeatedly between the Locators. Iterative Quantization gives a good result. If the result is too loud, reduce the velocity or apply compression in the Track Inspector.

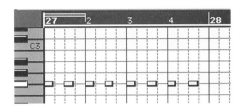

Figure 20.15 Take 9 – The Tambourine plays a one bar pattern.

• Save song – compare with project8/9.arr.

The final mix

A final mix can be seen and heard in project8.all (Figure 20.16).

Figure 20.16 proj8mix.all – a final mix.

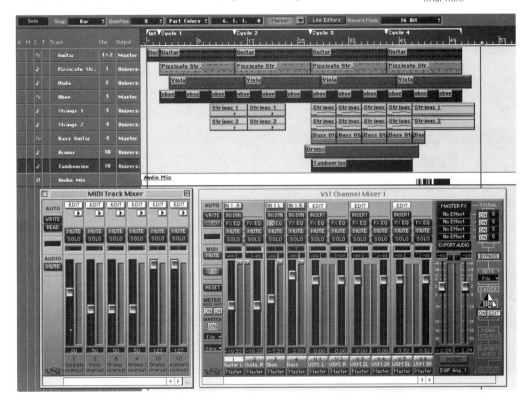

This is what I did.

I set the Outputs on the Universal Sound Module thus:

Pizzicato strings	MIDI Channel 1 to MIDI Outport 1
Viola	MIDI Channel 2 to MIDI Outport 1
Strings 1	MIDI Channel 3 to MIDI Outport 1
Drums	MIDI Channel 10 to MIDI Outport 2

I left their settings at a nominal level in the VST Channel Mixer and set their volume and pan in the MIDI Track Mixer.

I set pan and volume for Audio Tracks in the VST Channel Mixer. Bass guitar was placed conventionally, in the centre, as was the oboe.

TIP

You can beef up the bass part some more by lengthening the Attack time. Experiment!

One VST Send Effect is used – Reverb (pre-set Long and Warm) on the oboe. To beef things up a bit, VST Dynamics compression and limiting can be applied to the bass guitar. To do this:

- Click on the button marked DYN near the top of the Channel Strip to open the dynamics section (left).
- Turn on the button named Compress. It will illuminate.

- Set the threshold level to –35.0dB and the ratio to 4.0:1.

- Set the Attack level at 10.0ms and the Release control to Auto by activating the button named Auto. It will illuminate.

- At this setting, gain reduction will be something in the order of 12 – 15dB so make that up with the Make Up Gain control knob. Use a setting of 15.0 dB.

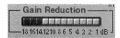

Play it through and you will notice the red clipping indicator is illuminating on the bass Channel. To solve this apply some limiting in the Limit section.

- Activate the Limit button and set the Threshold to around –5.00dB and activate the Auto Release button.
- Return to the Channel Mixer and reset the red clipping indicator (click on the red light to turn it off).
- Play the piece through again and the problem should be solved. A beefier Bass signal with the dangerous peak levels reduced.

Once everything was balanced OK I activated the Write button in the VST Channel Mixer and created a fade at the point where the procession was leaving our view. A new audio mix Track was created in the Arrange window.

Compress works just like any standard audio compressor by converting a large dynamic range into a smaller one. As you compress a signal the loud parts are reduced and the quieter parts are raised. In our case all signals below –35.0dB are unaffected. All signals above –35.0dB are compressed at a ratio of 4:1. In other words, for every 4dB that the signal rises above the threshold it will increase by only 1dB.

The attack control determines how soon compression kicks in above the set threshold and the release control how soon it returns to its original level.

Dance music 21

The influence of dance music on the media

Dance music started in the mid 1980s and nobody thought it would last. Here we are in the 21st century and it's still with us and getting stronger. Why is it so popular? Because people love dancing to it. More to the point, young people love dancing to it, and that's why it is being featured more and more in radio and TV commercials targeted specifically at the young. It also forms a backdrop to many sports, motoring, even wildlife programs on the 'telly' as well as frequent use in drama, soaps and films.

Of course, there are many styles within this genre – House, Garage, Trance, Drum & Bass, Hip Hop and Ambient, to name just a few – but when used as background music the actual style is not so important. What is important is the general impression that the product being plugged, or the program being watched, is cool and up to date! Unlike most dance music there is sometimes a strong melodic line and more harmonic movement involved but the key ingredient is always present: rhythm. Drum and bass loops being the most prominent.

There are many excellent loops available from companies such as PocketFuel, and these can often make a good starting point. I have made use of a PocketFuel loop myself in Project 9 (Chapter 22). Trawling through hundreds of loops can be time consuming and often it is quicker to make your own, particularly if you have a specific brief to work to. This is after all, far more creative. And where's an ideal place to construct loops? Cubase for one! Once you have made one or two, confidence grows, and before you know it you may well have a large library of your own original loops.

Constructing a drum and bass loop – how's it done?

Realism gives way to creativity when making loops, although it cannot be disregarded altogether. The most popular drum machines, such as the TR808 started life emulating acoustic kits, even though they are chosen for different reasons today. Bass drum, snare drum, toms and hi-hats are all present on acoustic kits and function the same way on virtual kits. The beauty of using them in dance music is the knowledge that they do not necessarily have to sound anything like a real drummer. We are limited only by our imagination. Having said that, control is needed. As in most creative forms, no matter how complicated, simplicity lies at the heart of things.

Here's a four bar loop to examine.

- Load loops/latloop.all from the CD and have a listen.
- Set the Output columns to the Universal Sound Module.

It's fast, frenetic and Latin in style. It doesn't belong to any particular dance music genre but would be a suitable starting point for a number of uses; a carnival scene maybe.

All percussion work was done in the Drum Edit window using the Drumstick Tool to enter the notes with a mouse. This is how I built it up.

1 I decided on a tempo – fast, frantic, Latin – 140 bpm seemed appropriate.

2 On Track 1, I created a Part between bar 1 and 5 in the Arrange window.

3 I selected the USM Standard Kit and loaded the General MIDI Drum Map.

4 On the Bass Drum line I entered a note on every beat of each bar. I chose a velocity value of 75 (Figure 21.1). To create a sense of urgency all the notes, except the first beat of bar 1, were shifted ahead of the beat by four ticks. There are various ways of doing this; perhaps the easiest is to enter –4 in the Track Inspector and from the Functions menu apply Freeze Play Parameters.

Figure 21.1 Track 1 – the Bass Drum.

5 On Track 2, I created another Part, and on the Pedal HiHat line entered a note on the second half of every beat. I chose a velocity value of 120 (Figure 21.2). Placing the notes between the bass drum adds to that sense of urgency required here.

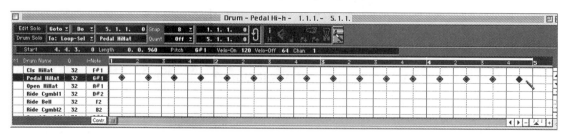

Figure 21.2 Track 2 the Hi-Hat.

6 On Track 3, I created another Part, and on the LowMid Tom line entered a simple pattern. A velocity value of 45 was used (Figure 21.3).

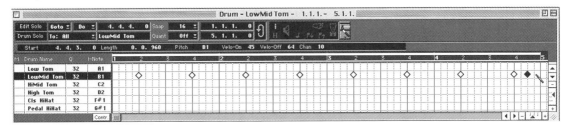

7 On Track 4, I created another Part, and on the El. Snare line entered a pattern between bars 1 and 3, then copied it between bars 3 and 5. A velocity value of 45 was used (Figure 21.4). It's the snare that brings this pattern alive. I kept it simple to begin with and...

Figure 21.3 Track 3 – the Low Mid Tom.

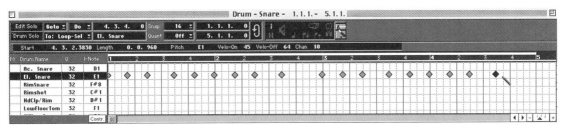

8 ...changed the snap value to 32 and created snare rolls. For realism, I drew a velocity ramp in the Controller section (Figure 21.5).

Figure 21.4 Track 4 – the Snare Drum.

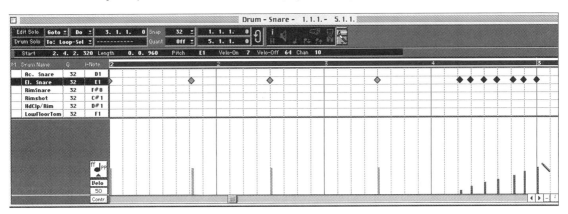

9 On Track 5, I created another Part, and on the High Agogo line, entered a pattern in bar 1 and copied it throughout the loop. A velocity of 45 was used (Figure 21.6).

Figure 21.5 Track 4 – the Snare Drum roll.

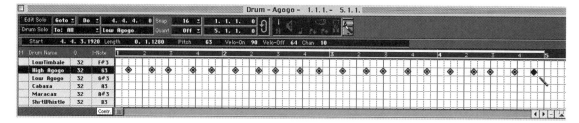

Figure 21.6 Track 5 – the High Agogo.

10 On Track 6, I created another Part, and on the Vibraslap line entered one note on the last sixteenth of bar 4. A velocity value of 120 was used. As each new cycle begins this has the effect of anticipating the first beat and adds to the urgency (Figure 21.7).

Figure 21.7 Track 6 – the Vibraslap.

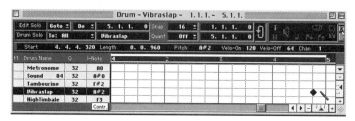

11 A meaty bass line was added. This was not entered with the mouse, but played in real time and left unquantized. Note how the bass was played ahead of the beat at bars 2, 3 and 4. This was a direct result of the bass drum being moved back; it influenced the way I played (Figure 21.8).

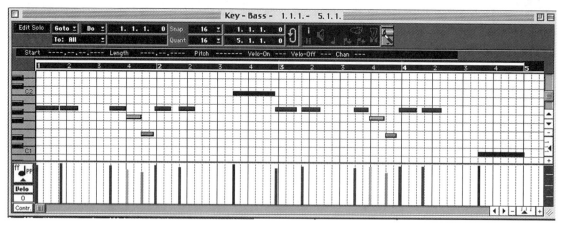

Figure 21.8 Track 7 – the Bass line.

12 Last but not least, to loosen things up a little, small amounts of randomization were applied to some of the Tracks in the Extended Track Inspector.

More could be done. Experiment with it yourself if you like. Adding effects will beef it up even more. Try the Phaser included with Cubase VST.

22

Project 9 – Get creative with Cubase jingle

Musical objectives
- To construct a jingle in dance music style.
- Improvise a vocal line using the phrase 'Get creative with Cubase'.

New Cubase skills
- Import and use a Recycle File.
- Utilize the VST Instrument – Neon.

Preparation
- From the CD, copy the folder named 'project9' folder to your computer.
- On your computer, create a folder called 'mywork9' or something similar in which to save your work.
- Open a New Arrangement [File>New Arrangement].
- On the Transport Bar, set the Time Signature to 4/4.
- Our tempo for this piece is 120 bpm. Set this in the Mastertrack if not already loaded by default.
- In the 'mywork9' folder, save as Song File myproj9.all or something similar.

The brief
Using a combination of audio loops and sequenced MIDI instruments compose a short jingle suitable for use with the 'Get creative' web site. Record a vocal track chanting or singing the words 'Get creative with Cubase'.

Quantize values are provided as a guide with this project but it will be best to leave the MIDI Parts un-quantized if possible.

If you want to listen through the finished Song file and find out how it goes load project9.all

You will need to set the Output columns to the VST Instruments called Universal Sound Module and Neon otherwise you may not hear anything! See the Appendix – Page 194 – for details.

Take 1

• Create a mono audio Track (Ch 1) and rename it 'Drums'.

> *Track Inspector*
> Mono
>
> *Transport Bar*
> Locators: (L) 1.1.1 (R) 2.1.1

If you have read chapters 9 and 10 – all about getting ideas and developing them – then you will understand the importance of knowing where you are heading. This is often best worked out away from the computer either in your head or sometimes as notes or sketches on paper.

Although the drum loop comes first in this project, it must be said that the idea for the vocal part came first. It was buzzing around in my head for weeks before I actually got around to recording it. Although it's the essence of the piece and everything else is built around it, for now, it can wait.

We are going to Import a ReCycle File – donated by Pocketfuel from their Steinberg RADS collection, Vol. 3 (www.pocketfuel.com).

• Ensure that the Locators are at the correct position and from the project9 folder import 89bpm.rex [File>Import>ReCycle File ...].

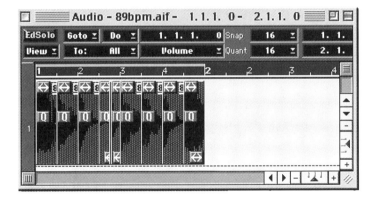

Figure 22.1 Pocketfuel's ReCycle file – 89bpm – seen here after conversion to an Audio file

A copy is made of the ReCycle file. This copy is converted to an audio file and added to the Audio Pool. Do not delete or move the original file.

The ReCycle file was exported from ReCycle at 89bpm. Our piece is set to 120 bpm. The ReCycled file will play back at any tempo. Try it!

• Repeat the Part (bars 1 – 2) seven times as far as bar 9.

We'll do a rough mix as we go so:

• In the VST Channel Mixer set the drums fairly high, around –3db.
• Save song – compare with project9/1.arr.

> ## INFO
>
> *When ReCycle files are imported, Cubase makes a copy which is converted to an audio file and added to the Audio Pool. It is important that the original ReCycle file is not moved or deleted. Why? If you later re-import the corresponding audio file Cubase 'remembers' the location of the original. If you've moved it, the audio file will not open.*

When loading *my* Cubase Arrange files into *your* Song file version for comparison, remember to:

1 Check that the Universal Sound Module and any other VST Instruments needed have been loaded.
2 Ensure the Output columns display the USM and any other VST Instruments needed.
3 To avoid confusion, close down *my* Arrange file version before any further saving of *your* Song file.

Take 2

• Create a MIDI Track (Ch 1) and rename it 'Bass'.

Track Inspector
Output: Cubase VST Instrument 'Neon'
Patchname: Deep Bass Fiths

Status Bar
Quantize [16]

Transport Bar
Locators: (L) 1.1.1 (R) 5.1.1

The Neon synthesizer, which is included with Cubase, is just what we need here to underpin the drum loop and a simple repetitive riff is all that's required (Figure 22.2), Let's try this one, it only uses three notes. Just the job.

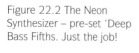
Figure 22.2 The Neon Synthesizer – pre-set 'Deep Bass Fifths. Just the job!

• Record the bass part between the Locators (Figure 22.3). If you can play it accurately, without quantization, then so much the better, if not use Iterative Quantize to tighten things up. Not too much though, this line needs 'feel'. Of course, what you see is not exactly what you get here because there is another line sounding one fifth below! If there isn't – check the Neon Preset in the Track Inspector.
• Repeat the Part (bars 1 – 5) once as far as bar 9.

Adjust the volume in the MIDI Track Mixer.

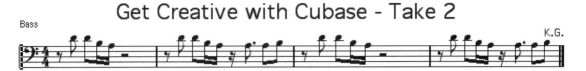

Bass

Get Creative with Cubase - Take 2

K.G.

Figure 22.3 Take 2 – record the Deep Bass Fifths.

- Save song – compare with project9/2.arr.

Start thinking about where in the piece to put the *Get creative with Cubase* vocal line. Try improvising, either singing or chanting, along with the track. Even in this short space of nine bars there are endless possibilities. I know how my mine goes, it's been driving me nuts for days! However, before my forthcoming virtuoso vocal performance, let's add another short loop. This time its funky guitar.

Take 3

> *Track Inspector*
> Stereo
>
> *Transport Bar*
> Locators: (L) 5.1.1 (R) 6.1.1

- Create a stereo audio Track (Ch 3+4) and rename it 'Guitar'.
- Ensure that the Locators are at the correct position and from your mywork9 folder open guitar.prt.
- Repeat the Part (bars 5 – 6) between bars 7 – 8.
- In the VST Channel Mixer, adjust the volume to around –7db.

- Save song – compare with project9/3.arr.

OK, we have a nice funky background as a basis for the vocal, bars 1 – 5 serving as an introduction. We will now record the vocal. As I'm not too hot at singing, I decided to record my version in two takes, the first being 'Get creative' and the second 'with Cubase.' This served my purposes fine because I wanted the phrase split up to sound between each guitar loop.

At this point in the project you have the choice of recording your own improvised vocal or loading the audio files provided. It may be better to continue with mine (if you can stand it!) and overdub yours later.

Take 4

- Create a mono audio Track (Ch 5) and rename it 'Vocal'.

> *Track Inspector*
> Mono
>
> *Transport Bar*
> Locators: (L) 5.1.1 (R) 7.1.1

- Ensure that the Locators are at the correct position and from the project9 folder open vocal_1.prt.
- Change the Locators to (L) 7.1.1 (R) 9.1.1 and ensure that the Locators are at the correct position and from the project9 folder open vocal_2.prt. Its most likely that another Track will be created containing the new Part. Simply move it to the correct position on the first vocal Track and delete the unwanted Track afterwards.
- In the VST Channel Mixer set the volume at around 0.00db.

- Save song – compare with project9/4.arr (Figure 22.4).

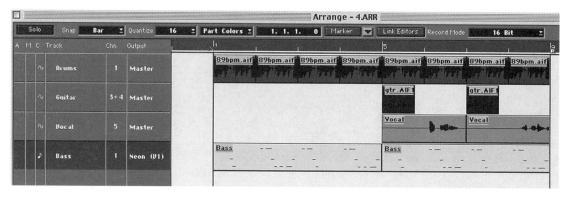

Figure 22.4 *Get creative with Cubase* 4.arr – the picture so far.

Obviously this has to now move on, but quite how long is still unknown so:

- Select the drum Parts between bars 7 – 9 and repeat it 10 times as far as bar 29.
- Select the bass Part between bars 5 – 9 and repeat it five times as far as bar 29.

This gives us a decent length to work in and will probably be all that is needed before we loop the entire piece. The vocal can stand another repeat before boredom sets in and the same goes for the guitar so:

- Select the guitar and vocal Parts between bars 5 – 9 and repeat them once.

- Save song – compare with project9/4a.arr.

I can hear this Hank Marvin (60s guitar hero!) twangy guitar style riff in my head. I don't play guitar, and I couldn't find the right sound in the General MIDI sounds of the Universal Sound Module until I came across the sitar sample. Played low enough it sounds pretty close to the sound I want. This may well be out of the sitar's normal range, I haven't checked, but the effect is right and I'm prepared to take a liberty.

Take 5

• Create a MIDI Track (Ch 2) and rename it 'Sitar'.

Track Inspector
Output: USM
Program: 105
Patchname: Sitar

Status Bar
Quantize [16]

Transport Bar
Locators: (L) 6.1.1 (R) 8.1.1

• Record the guitar part between the Locators (Figure 22.5). Yes it's only one note but Hank was very fond of, and indeed famous for, using his tremolo arm to bend notes, and that's what I want here. To achieve this start the note one tone lower using the pitch bend device on your MIDI keyboard, and slide up to the correct pitch approximately eighth note later. It will be made easier if you restrict the pitch bend range to two (semitones) in the Universal Sound Module itself (Figure 22.6).

Figure 22.5 Take 5 – record the sitar.

Get Creative with Cubase - Take 5   K.G.

Sitar!

Play D1 and slide to E1

• Repeat the sitar Part (bars 6 – 8) 10 times as far as bar 28.
• In the MIDI Track Mixer, adjust the volume to about 60.

• Save song – compare with project9/5.arr.

Apart from the intro (bars 1 – 5) the vocal between bars 5 – 13 has run out of steam. Before introducing something new it may be effective to repeat just the second phrase along with the guitar so:

• Select the guitar and vocal Parts between bars 11 – 13 and repeat them once only.

• Save song – compare with project9/5a.arr.

Figure 22.6 USM Pitch Bend Range restricted to 2 semitones.

It's time for something new. Repetition and variation, remember. The drums and bass can chug on but we must introduce another element or two. We'll start with a moody synth line, something simple that first climbs and then descends.

Take 6

Track Inspector
Output: USM
Program: 97
Patchname: FX 1 (rain)

Status Bar
Quantize [16]

Transport Bar
Locators: (L) 15.1.1 (R) 23.1.1

Figure 22.7 Take 6 – record
the synth part; FX1 (rain).

- Create a MIDI Track (Ch 3) and rename it 'Synth FX 1'.
- Record the synth part between the Locators (Figure 22.7). Play it freely and leave the result un-quantized. Things have now taken a

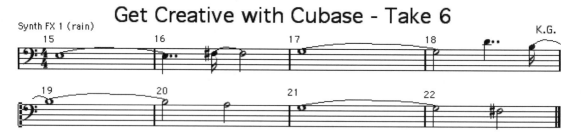

new direction with the synth creating a degree of tension.
- In the MIDI Track Mixer adjust the volume to about 64.

- Save song – compare with project9/6.arr.

I'm rather fond of simple two note string pads for adding a touch of mystery. Placing one behind the moving synth line will further establish the change of mood at measure 15.

Take 7

- Create a MIDI Track (Ch 4) and rename it 'Synth Strings'.

Track Inspector
Output: USM
Program: 51
Patchname: SynthStrings 1

Status Bar
Quantize [8]

Transport Bar
Locators: (L) 15.1.1 (R) 23.1.1

- Record the string pad in Figure 22.8. Use a light touch and if need be, reduce the velocity of the notes in the Track Inspector.

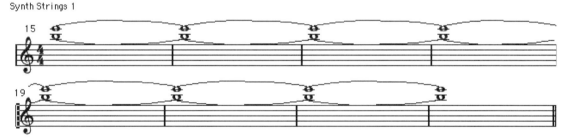

Get Creative with Cubase - Take 7

K.G.

- In the MIDI Track Mixer keep the volume very low, around 10.

- Save song – compare with project9/7.arr.

Figure 22.8 Take 7 – record the string pad.

There's room for something else over those synth parts. Ask yourself what you can add. Sit back and listen. What comes to mind? You may well play guitar or some other instrument. If so it's time to 'Get creative' and add something of your own. It is important though to try and hear what the piece needs first, before doodling commences. It need only be something very simple. What did I think of? Well I play saxophone and a very short jazz be-bop motif kept nagging away in my head. It refused to budge and so I recorded it.

As with the vocal part, at this point in the project you have the choice of recording your own instrument. You may prefer to continue with my soprano sax and overdub something of your own later.

Take 8

- Create a Mono Audio Track (Ch 6) and rename it 'Soprano'.

Track Inspector
Mono
Snap (1/2)

Transport Bar
Locators: (L) 15.3.1 (R) 17.3.1

- Ensure that the Locators are at the correct position and from the project9 folder open soprano.prt.
- Repeat the Part (bars 15.3.1 – 17.3.1) three times as far as bar 23.3.1.

- Save song – compare with project9/8.arr.

- Set the Locators to (L) 1.1.1 (R) 23.1.1 and activate the cycle button. That's long enough for our purposes. Each cycle lasts 44 seconds.

The mix
Load project9.all to view and hear a mix of *Get creative with Cubase*.

Mixer devices
The Arrange window appears with a view of the two mixer devices used: The MIDI Track Mixer – used to control the volume and pan information of the MIDI Tracks. The VST Channel Mixer – used to control all aspects of the Audio Tracks, the effects and EQ for the VST Instruments USM and Neon as well as volume for the Neon.

Send Effects
The Send Effects used are:

DoubleDelay – preset: half note left right – put to good use on the guitar where it has plenty of room to sound between each guitar Part.
Reverb – preset: Long and Warm – used on the vocal.

Figure 22.9 Double Delay is put to good use on guitar.

EQ is used on: Neon (Bass). The Boost Bass preset was used as a starting point – to do just that – and modified a little (Figure 22.10).

Figure 22.10 EQ is used on Neon.

- Open the VST Channel Mixer [Panels>VST Channel Mixer] and click on one of the EQ buttons above the Channel Strip for Neon 1 and 2. The Channel Settings window will open.
- In the Channel Settings window choose the Boost Bass pre-set in the EQ section.

- From here experiment with the EQ curve by clicking on the display. This will activate a numbered handle which can be dragged around to alter both gain and frequency simultaneously.

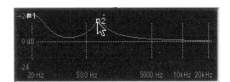

Gain – affects the amount of boost or cut around a set frequency.
Frequency – the centre frequency for the equalization. Around this frequency, the sound will be boosted or cut depending on the Gain.
Q – determines the width of the frequency band around the centre frequency.

For more info about the EQ section, refer to your *Getting into the Details* document on the Cubase CD.

EQ
EQ – posh term for tone control! Seriously though, there is so much tosh talked about EQ. So what exactly is it? Well, gain control, as we all know, increases or decreases signal levels. EQ control is much the same except that it only operates on a specific area of the acoustic spectrum.

Think of a basic hi-fi system. The treble and bass controls operate only on their respective areas. However more control is needed for recording, and the middle control was invented to provide gain at the middle of the acoustic spectrum without interfering with the treble and bass.

Next came the sweep controls allowing the frequency range affected by the mid control to be finely tuned. But that wasn't enough. Another control was devised to define the width of the frequency band. The name for this new three control equalizer? Parametric EQ, and that's what we have included with Cubase VST.

Compression was used carefully on the vocal before treatment with 'Doppler' (see below). Settings used – ratio of 2:1 threshold: –31dB attack: 10.5ms (Figure 22.11).

Compression can also be applied to the Neon (bass) via the Channel Insert section.

Figure 22.11 (left) Careful use of Compression on the vocal ...

Figure 22.12 ...and (right) on Neon, via the Channel Insert section.

• Click on the Insert button at the top of the Neon Channel Strip (left). This will open the Channel Settings window.
• Within the Channel Settings window, in the section headed Inserts load CubaseDynamics from the drop-down menu.
• Activate the On button and click on the Edit button. The Channel Insert section opens.
• Try these settings as a starting point:

ratio	3:1
threshold	–38.0dB
attack	54.2ms
release	Auto
make up gain	9.0dB

Load CubaseDynamics

But don't forget to experiment!

The USM MIDI Channels are all routed to Output 1 – no effects are used so there's no need to split them. Their volume and pan settings are controlled from the MIDI Track Mixer.

By now I expect you have noticed the extra Track (muted) entitled 'Doppler Vocal'. You will remember that this piece evolved from the phrase 'Get creative with Cubase' and that it had been rattling around in my head for some time before it was recorded. Well this is how I actually heard it. I could never sing it this way – or any other way, come to that – so I treated the Track afterwards with the help of Steinberg's 'Doppler' a VST Plug-In included with their GRM Tools Vol. 2. A great bit of kit.

Doppler simulates the effect of a sound moving towards or away from you and this also gives rise to an apparent change of pitch. Many strange effects are possible with a little experimentation.

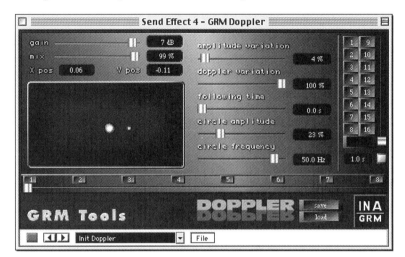

Figure 22.13 Steinberg's VST PlugIn 'Doppler'.

23 Knowing the score

To examine the Cubase files for this chapter: From the CD, copy the folder named 'scores' to your computer.

Rebecca's got the job. She's been sending demos and making follow up calls to a small independent TV production company in her area for some time now and they have finally given her a chance. They sent her a video. She composed some music using Cubase VST, mastered it to DAT and dropped it off personally. 'Great,' they said. 'How about a live version, played by real musicians?'

'No problem', replied Rebecca, I can print the score and parts direct from Cubase. 'We'll book the studio and hire the session musicians,' they said. Rebecca went home a very happy person indeed.

A week later Rebecca arrives at the studio and peers through the control room window at the motley bunch of musicians sitting around drinking cups of coffee and reading newspapers. Scraps of conversation can be heard through the studio monitors. 'My central heating has bust again… I still haven't been paid for the last session we did here …'

Rebecca hands out the printed parts and listens nervously as the band begins a run through. 'It doesn't sound too good,' she thinks, 'I thought these guys could read and play anything that's put in front of them'. Pretty soon the band grinds to a halt. 'These parts are useless,' exclaims a particularly belligerent trumpet player. 'My part hasn't even been transposed.' We've all got different note lengths', says the trombonist. 'My dog could write better parts than this!' says the drummer.

So what did she do wrong? Although Rebecca can play piano, compose tunes and arrange them in Cubase, her music reading and writing skills lack professionalism. She made the all too common mistake of thinking that the notes she actually played into Cubase would appear correctly in the Score Printing and Layout section of the program. What she had not realised is that, in order for the music to be readable by musicians, some editing is required. She played the original sequenced version to the musicians and after correcting the parts, they played it perfectly. Of course this took up valuable studio time and the session over ran by 15 minutes. Overtime had to be paid to the musicians and studio owners.

How Cubase VST Score Edit works

The Score Edit section of Cubase varies considerably between Cubase VST and Cubase Score or Cubase VST/32. Basically, the ordinary VST version is much more limiting in its layout and printing features than the other two versions. For serious layout and printing facilities use either the Score or VST/32 versions.

It is important to understand the relationship between Score Edit and the rest of the program. To begin with, it will not display the notes of recorded audio data. Not for the time being anyway. Maybe one day the technology will be able to handle it. No, Cubase Score interprets recorded MIDI data and according to the settings you make, displays the result as conventional music notation.

Before editing, every note recorded as MIDI data in Cubase is faithfully displayed in the Score Editor exactly as it was played. For example four bars of Jingle Bells – load score/jingle.all/jingle1.arr – captured in Cubase displays like this (Figure 23.1).

Looks wrong, doesn't it? But, play it through and it sounds OK (don't forget to set the Output column to the Universal Sound Module). The same data, after a little tweaking in the Staff Settings dialogue box (Figure 23.2) looks like Figure 23.3 – score/jingle.all/jingle2.arr – a perfect display. The MIDI data hasn't changed, just the interpretation.

Figure 23.1 Jingle Bells – looks wrong doesn't it?

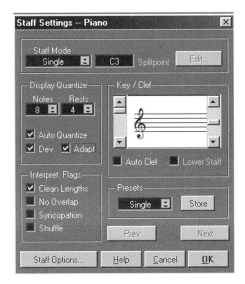

Figure 23.2 ...after some tweaking in the Staff Settings dialogue ...

Figure 23.3 ...a perfect display.

This book is not a manual. At this point I would advise those readers who are unfamiliar with Cubase Score to study the *Score.pdf* document that is supplied with the program and work through the tutorials contained in it. Afterwards, proceed to the next chapter in this book, where a good many of the commonly used Score Edit features are used to format the music recorded in Project 6.

Project 10 – Score clean-up

24

Musical objectives
- To transform an unintelligible mess into a readable score!

New Cubase skills
- Use the Staff Settings dialogue to: determine staff mode, key signature and clef – choose Display Quantize and Interpretation Flag options for a clean score and correct notation – automatically display a transposed trumpet part.
- Use the Merge Tracks feature to create a single drum Track from three separate Tracks.
- Use Staff Preset feature to create a drum Staff.
- Use the Make Chords feature to automatically calculate and insert guitar chords.
- Use the Fixed Note feature and Note Info dialogue to create 'slash style' chord symbols for the guitar part.
- Use the Symbol Palettes to insert slurs, accents, rehearsal marks, text and other markings.
- Use the Tool Bar to hide notes and rests and insert accidentals.
- Use the Layout Settings dialogue to – Create a Score Layout – Insert brackets to separate the brass and rhythm sections.
- Create a Pick-up Bar.
- Insert title and copyright details.

Preparation
- From the CD, copy the folder named 'project10' to your computer.
- Create a folder called 'mywork10' or something similar in which to save your work.

The brief
The football theme, commissioned in Project 6, was a success. However, the program makers would like a studio version, played by real musicians. You need to prepare a score and printed parts for the session.

Because some of the work required to produce a presentable score may well involve some destructive editing we are going to work on a copy of the original. Use the example on the CD – project10/pr6_copy.arr – as the basis for your work.

- Load project10/pr6_copy.arr and in your 'mywork10' folder, save as Song File – myproj10.all or something similar.

If you have already worked through Project 6 – A Football Theme – you will remember that it contained an audio Track featuring yours truly on tenor sax. This has been deleted. It was an improvised overdub and will not need scoring anyway. Besides, the company commissioning the music prefer the alternative solo trumpet (there's no accounting for taste!).

- Rename the three brass Tracks as Trumpets 1, 2 and 3.

Figure 24.1 Rename the brass Tracks as Trumpet 1, 2 and 3.

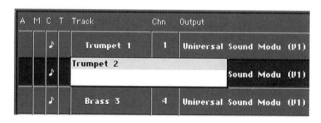

Compare with project10/1.arr.

Figure 24.2 Mmm ... it doesn't look quite right somehow.

- Select Track 1/Trumpet 1 (not the Parts) and open the score. [Edit>Score] (Figure 24.2).

- From within the Score select Page Mode. [Score>Page Mode] From now on, when working on this score, use Page Mode.

What do you think? Your answers will vary according to how much knowledge of music notation you have. If you can't read music at all it will not make much sense. In this case some time studying music theory is the only course of action open to you if you want to work with Cubase Score.

If you have experience of reading music at an entry or intermediate level, your answer might be: 'Looks all right to me. The first note is F followed by Bb and C. Yes I can understand that. Not sure about the rhythm though. It looks a bit funny.' In your case this project will help you display a decent, readable score.

If you are an experienced music reader your reaction will probably be something like: 'Well it is difficult to read because the key signature is missing and the note lengths are incorrectly displayed. There are no dynamic or articulation markings either.'

If you are a professional trumpet player your reaction may well be something like: 'Surely you don't expect me to read this rubbish!'

- From the Score Editor open Staff Settings [Score>Staff Settings]. A dialogue box appears.
- In the Staff Mode section, ensure that 'Single' is selected.

The first things to change are the Display Quantize options. Our smallest note value in this piece is an eighth note so:

- Select that option in the Note pop-up menu.
- Select 4 from the Rest pop-up menu. Cubase will now display only rests smaller than this value where absolutely necessary.

We can leave the Auto Quantize box unchecked in this case. The Interpretation Flags are also unnecessary here.

- In the Key/Clef Box, change the key to Bb (two flats). The treble clef should be displayed already. If not, change it.

The Staff Settings dialogue should now look like those in Figure 24.3.

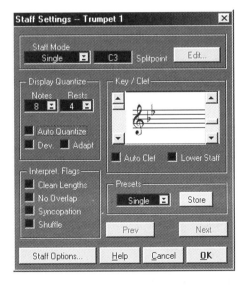

Figure 24.3 Staff Settings for trumpet 1.

- Close the dialogue box. Yes, things are considerably improved. Gone are all the messy sixteenth notes and rests for starters.
- Save song – compare with project10/2.arr (Figure 24.4).

Figure 24.4 It's a big improvement. Gone are the messy sixteenth notes and rests.

- Select the Trumpet 2 and 3 Tracks in turn (not the Parts) and perform the same functions on those Tracks.

- Save song – compare with project10/3.arr.

- Select the Bass Track (not the Parts) and open the score. Oh dear! This is enough to drive any self respecting bass player completely crackers! It's a jumble. Parts like this have been handed out though, believe me! (Figure 24.5).

Figure 24.5 A bass player's nightmare!

- From the Score, open the Staff Settings and as with the Trumpet Tracks, change the Display Quantize options to Notes: 8 and Rests: 4.
- Alter the key to Bb and this time select the bass clef.
- Close the dialogue box. What a difference! (Figure 24.6).

Figure 24.6 What a difference!

- Save song – compare with project10/4.arr.

- Return to the Arrange Page.

Conventional scores do not have separate drum staves. We have two, kick and snare drum Tracks plus a whistle on the Referee Track. Let's combine them.

- Ensure that the General MIDI Drum Map is loaded [File>Open from Library>General MIDI Drum Map].
- Mute all Tracks except kick, snare and Referee.
- Set the Locators to (L) 1. 1. 1 (R) 37. 1. 1.
- Create a new Track [Structure>Create Track] and rename it Drums. Set Channel to 10.
- With the new drum Track selected, merge the un-muted Tracks [Structure>Merge Tracks]. A new Part entitled Merged should now appear on the drum Track (Figure 24.7).

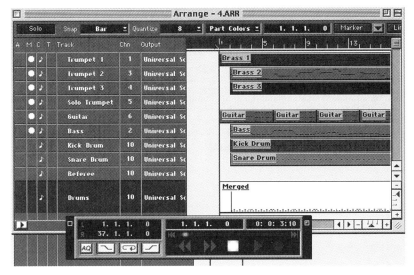

Figure 24.7 A new Part – 'Merged' – appears on the Drum Track.

- Open the score and select the drum staff Preset [Score>Staff Presets>Drums] If the General MIDI Drum Map has been loaded the drum clef will appear along with conventional drum notation – kick drum: first space, and snare: third space on the staff (Figure 24.8).

Figure 24.8 Conventional drum notation – kick drum: first space, snare: third space

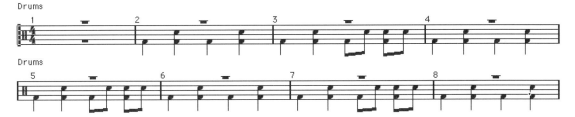

- Open the Staff Settings dialogue and you will see that the Display Quantize options have been set to Notes: 16 and Rests: 4. Auto Quantize has been checked but can be turned off if you like as there are no triplets around. Leave Clean Lengths checked (turn it off and you will see why!)

Don't worry about the referee disappearing off the pitch! (bars 35 and 36) – we'll get him back later.

- Close the score, delete the old drums and Referee Tracks and un-mute the muted Tracks.

- Save song – compare with project10/5.arr.

Figure 24.9 We can't give that to a guitarist! ...

- Select the guitar Track (not the Parts) and open the score (Figure 24.9).

Well we can't give that to a guitar player. He'll fall about laughing! What he requires here is a chord sheet. How do we do that? There are various methods. Here's one way to do it.
- Open Staff Settings and change the Display Quantize options to Notes: 8 and Rests: 4.
- Check the Clean Lengths box.
- Change the key to Bb.
- Check the Syncopation box. This cleans up all the notes that are tied across the beat.

Figure 24.10 ...that's better.

Compare to Figure 24.10.

- By clicking on the Make Chords symbol on the Tool Bar or using the 'Do' pop-up menu (Figure 24.11) we can insert chord symbols above the changes. This also inserts the bass note of the chord. However in our case this is superfluous. So whilst performing Make Chords press Ctrl on your computer keyboard (Command on the Mac) to insert chords without unnecessary bass notes.

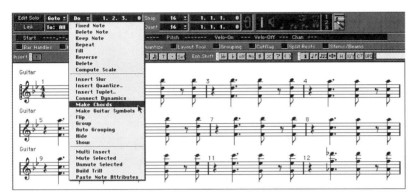

Figure 24.11 Use the 'Do' pop-up menu to insert chords automatically.

The chords are inserted and left selected. Whilst still selected move them away from the notes to the begriming of each bar, for clarity (appropriate in this case because we have only one chord per bar).

- Save song – compare with project10/6.arr Figure (24.12)

Figure 24.12 The chords are inserted above the notes but can be repositioned

Things are much clearer but we don't need the note display as well as chord symbols. We could leave them; it doesn't really matter. Although a little time consuming it's better to delete them.

- Delete all the notes except the bottom note on each stem.
- Select the 1st note (F3) and from the 'Do' pop-up menu, choose 'Fixed Note' and from the 'To' pop-up menu choose 'All'. All notes are now changed to F.
- Select All [Edit>Select>Select All] and double click any note head. A Note Info dialogue box appears.
- Change the Note Head option to a slash symbol (/) and click 'Apply.' All the note heads change to a slash symbol (Figure 24.13).

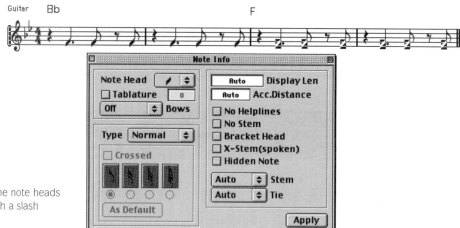

Figure 24.13 The note heads are replaced with a slash symbol.

- Save song – compare with project10/7.arr.

Figure 24.14 Select an accent from the Note Symbol Palette

Musicians need more than just notes on the staff to correctly interpret a written piece of music. Articulation markings are particularly important.

- Return to the trumpet 1 Track and open the score.
- Click on the first note in bar 34 (Bb4). A glance at the Info line above will tell you that this note received more velocity than the note following. So did the note at 34. 2. 3. 320 (Ab4). They were clearly accented and we need to point this out to the trumpet player, so:
- Select an accent (>) from the Note Symbol Palette [Score>Symbol Palettes>Note Symbols] and apply it to those notes by clicking on their note heads (Figure 24.14).

- Save song – compare with project10/8.arr.

On viewing project10/8.arr you will see that other accents and markings from the Note Symbol Palette have been applied.

The slurs in bar 34 were added by first selecting the notes and using the 'Do' pop-up menu (Figure 24.15).

Although not strictly necessary, but courteous, the first note in bar 14 has been given a natural sign (cautionary accidental). This was applied by first selecting the note and clicking the '?' button on the Tool Bar (Figure 24.16).

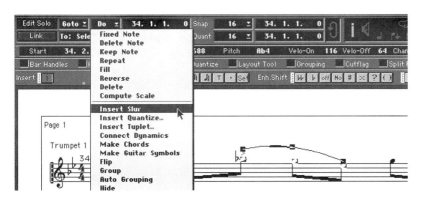

Figure 24.15 Use the 'Do' pop-up menu to insert slurs.

Figure 24.16 A cautionary accidental applied by selecting the note and clicking the '?' button.

- Change your version accordingly and Save Song.
- Return to the bass Track and open the score. The very last note is out of the bass player's range (it was played here on a synth). Move it an octave higher. Close score.
- Return to the dum Track and open the score. Time to get the Referee back on the pitch by dragging him up to the top line of the stave. A cymbal note head appears so we indicate to the player that a whistle is required by entering text [Score>Symbol Palettes>Other>Text] (Figure 24.17).
- Save song – compare with project10/9.arr.

- In the Arrange Page, glue all the Parts on their respective Tracks together. Rename the new Parts to match their Track names i.e.

Figure 24.17 We tell the drummer to blow his whistle!

Merged becomes Drums (this is purely for the sake of tidiness and not strictly necessary. Omit this step if you wish).

- Save song – compare with project10/10.arr.

In the Arrange window, Select All [Edit>Select>Select All].

- Open the score. From the score, open the Layout Settings dialogue box [Score>Layout Settings...] (Figure 24.18).

Figure 24.18 We create a
Score Layout using the Layout
Settings dialogue.

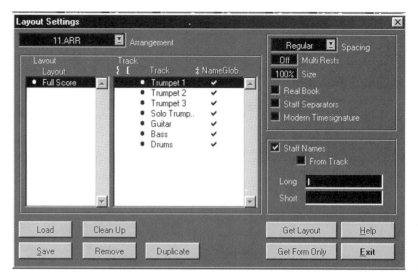

- Remove (with the Remove button) anything that shows in the Layout (left) and Track (right) windows. We are going to create a Layout for the full score, so:
- Press the 'Select Form Only' button – the dialogue box closes.
- Re-open it. Cubase has named the Layout 'Trumpet 1' (left) and ticked the selected Tracks (right).
- Rename the Layout 'Full Score' and press Exit to close the box.

You can now call up the 'Full Score' layout at any time:

> from the Score [Score>Display Layout>Full Score]
> from the Arrange Page [Edit>Select>Score Layout>Full Score]

- Save song – compare with project10/11.arr.

We are almost finished with the score. Just a few details to tidy up.

- Select the Full Score layout
- You may prefer to choose a landscape setting to view the score [File>Page Setup]. If printed it will look better this way.
- Clicking on the title at the top of the score will reveal a Title/Copyright dialogue box. Enter the details; in this case Title – Football Theme, Author – Keith Gemmell.

- Save song – compare with project10/12.arr.

On viewing project10/12.arr you will see that a number of other changes have taken place.
   Double bar lines have been inserted at the beginning of bars 2 and 18 (Double Click on bar line for menu) (Figure 24.19).
   The brass and rhythm sections have been bracketed (Figure 24.20). This can be done with the Layout Symbols Palette. However these were

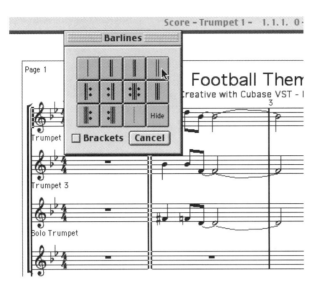

Figure 24.19 Double bar lines were inserted.

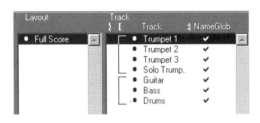

Figure 24.20 Brackets were inserted using the Layout Settings dialogue.

added in the Layout Settings dialogue. In the Track list there are columns for 'Braces' and 'Brackets'. Click in a column and drag downwards to select a group of Tracks.

The solo trumpet has been instructed to play an octave higher [Score>Symbol Palettes>Layout>System Text] (Figure 24.21).

Figure 24.21 The solo trumpet player is told to play 1 octave higher.

Helpful rehearsal letters A and B have been inserted at bars 2 and 18 [Score>Symbol Palettes>Layout>A] (Figure 24.22).

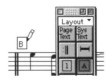

Figure 24.22 Helpful rehearsal markings were inserted.

Further refinements can be made in Score Preferences [Edit> Preferences>Score]. More can be done but by now I'm sure you've got the picture.

TIP

Transposing the Trumpet Part will also transpose that Part on the Full Score. To view the Full Score at concert pitch, transpose it back again.

INFO

Some writers prefer a transposed score, with all the instruments viewed in the keys in which the actual players will read them. Others, myself included, prefer to view their scores in concert pitch.

• Change your version accordingly and save song.

We will now prepare the trumpet 1 part. A portrait setting is the best view for this [File>Page Setup...]. There will be fewer pages than in landscape form. From the player's point of view, this is a good thing.

If you read Chapter 23 'Knowing the Score' you will remember the trumpet player complaining that his part had not been transposed. Our trumpet 1 part is in Bb at the moment. It will have to be transposed up a tone for performance purposes.

• Select the Trumpet 1 Track.
• Select Page Mode, open Staff Settings... and press the Staff Options... button. Another dialogue box appears.
• From the Instrument pop-up menu, select Trumpet. Close the boxes and hey presto! the Trumpet 1 score has been transposed to the key of C.

• Save song – compare with project10/13.arr.

On viewing the Trumpet part in project10/13.arr you will see that a number of other changes have taken place:

• Double bars have been inserted at bar 2 and 18.
• Track Names have been removed (uncheck them in the Layout Settings... dialogue box).
• Text – Trumpet 1 – has been added at the top left corner of the page. [Score>Symbols Palettes>Layout>Page Text].
• Rehearsal letters A and B have been inserted.
• A new Layout – Trumpet 1 – has been created.

• Change your version accordingly and Save Song.

The first bar contains unnecessary rests. It's really a pick-up bar. To modify it:

• Hide the rests with 'H' from the Tool Bar (Figure 24.23) and drag the bar line to the left.

Figure 24.23 Hide the rests in the 'pick-up' bar.

- Re-position the notes using the Layout Tool (Figure 24.24).

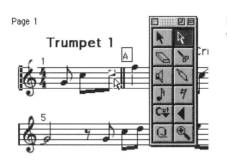

Figure 24.24 Reposition notes with the Layout Tool.

- Click on the Bar 1 number. A dialogue box opens (Figure 24.5). Enter an offset of −1. The pick-up bar is now set to 0. This can be hidden with the 'H' symbol on the Tool Bar.

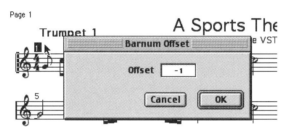

Figure 24.5 Enter an offset of −1.

- Save song – compare with project10.14.arr.

Appendix 1
VST Instrument checklist

All the MIDI content in all the Cubase Song Files uses the Universal Sound Module with just a few exceptions (see below).

When loading a Song file (.all) fresh from the CD, the Universal Sound Module will always be loaded. This can be confirmed by viewing the VST Instrument rack [Panels>VST Instruments]. Any other VST Instruments needed for the Song will also be seen here.

Although the correct Patch Name and Program Numbers will be displayed in the Arrange windows, the Output column, depending on your personal set-up and soundcard, may well display another General MIDI sound source. To hear the Song File as intended, change the Output to the Universal Sound Module.

A few Song Files also use the VST Instruments LM-9 and Neon. Here then is a check list to use when loading Song Files off the CD.

blocks.all
all MIDI Tracks USM

cells.all
all MIDI Tracks USM

exile.all
all MIDI Tracks USM

form.all
all MIDI Tracks USM

flutes.all
all MIDI Tracks USM

groove.all
all MIDI Tracks USM

horns.all
all MIDI Tracks USM

hodges.all
all MIDI Tracks USM

jingle.all
all MIDI Tracks USM

jitter.all
all MIDI Tracks USM

latloop.all
all MIDI Tracks USM

lick.all
all MIDI Tracks USM

minimal.all
all MIDI Tracks USM

project1.all
all MIDI Tracks USM

project2.all
All MIDI Tracks USM except Tracks 5 – 6 which use the LM-9

project3.all
all MIDI Tracks USM except Tracks 7 – 9 which use the LM-9

project4.all
All MIDI Tracks USM

project5.all
all MIDI Tracks USM

project6.all
all MIDI Tracks USM except Tracks 7+ 8 which use the LM-9

project7.all
all MIDI Tracks USM except Tracks 3 – 5 which use the LM-9

project8.all
all MIDI Tracks USM

project9.all
all MIDI Tracks USM except Track 5 which uses Neon (BassFiths)

strings.all
all MIDI Tracks USM

timpani.all
all MIDI Tracks USM

Appendix 2
Useful keyboard shortcuts

Throughout this book, for clarity, all Cubase Functions are referred to using the program's Menus. Power users can speed things up by using the many keyboard shortcuts available. For example the instruction 'Quantize' is followed by the Menu command in square brackets: [Functions>Quantize]. The equivalent key command is Q. Much quicker!

PC	Mac	Function
File Menu		
Ctrl O	Command O	Open File
Ctrl N	Command N	New Arrangement
Ctrl W	Command W	Close File
Ctrl S	Command S	Save Song
Ctrl Q	Command Q	Quit
Edit Menu		
Ctrl Z	Command Z	Undo
Ctrl X	Command X	Cut
Ctrl C	Command C	Copy
Ctrl V	Command V	Paste
Del		Delete Parts
	Command A	Select All
Ctrl E	Command E	Open Key Edit
Ctrl G	Command G	Open List Edit
Ctrl D	Command D	Open Drum Edit
Ctrl R	Command R	Open Score Edit
Ctrl M	Command M	Open Graphical Mastertrack
Shift Ctrl M	Shift Command M	Open List Mastertrack
Ctrl B	Command B	Open Notepad

PC	Mac	Function
Structure Menu		
Ctrl T	Command T	Create Track (Between Locators)
Ctrl P	Command P	Create Part (Between Locators)
Ctrl K	Command K	Repeat Part(s)
Functions Menu		
Q	Q	Quantize
U	U	Undo Quantize
Ctrl L	Command L	Open Logical Edit
Ctrl H	Command H	MIDI Functions>Transpose/Velocity
Alt T	Option T	MIDI Functions>Note Length
Panels Menu		
Ctrl [Num] *	Command *	Open VST Channel Mixer
Ctrl [Num] +	Command +	Open VST Master Mixer
	Command =	Open VST Send Effects
	Command /	Open VST Master Effects
Ctrl F	Command F	Open Audio Pool
Windows Menu		
F12	F12	Hides/Show Transport Bar
Alt Ctrl		Place Transport Bar Centre Screen
Arrange/Editors		
Alt M	Option M	Mute Selected Track
Alt N	Option N	Name Track/Drum
Alt J	Option J	Name Instrument
S	S	Solo on/off
Ctrl Shift T		Set Track Class
1	1	Quantize to Whole Note
2	2	Quantize to 1/2 Note
3	3	Quantize to 1/4 Note
4	4	Quantize to 1/8th Note
5	5	Quantize to 1/16 Note
6	6	Quantize to 32nd Note
7	7	Quantize to 64th Note

PC	Mac	Function
8	8	Quantize to 128th Note
T	T	Quantize to Triplet on/off
.	.	Quantize to Dotted on/off
Shift H	Shift H	Zoom In Vertical
Shift G	Shift G	Zoom Out Vertical
H	H	Zoom In Horizontal
G	G	Zoom Out Horizontal
Ctrl Left	Command Left	Nudge Event Left (Snap Value)
Ctrl Right	Command Right	Nudge Event Right (Snap Value)
Ctrl Up	Command Up	Nudge Event Up
Ctrl Down	Command Down	Nudge Event Down
Alt L	Option L	Set Left Loop
Alt R	Option R	Set Right Loop
Alt C	Option C	Controller Display On/Off
Alt I	Option I	Note Info On/Off
Alt O	Option O	Loop On/Off
Alt S	Option S	Drum Solo (Drum Editor)
A	A	Edit Solo
X	X	Sync on/off
C	C	Click on/off
L	L	Edit Left Locator
R	R	Edit Right Locator
P	P	Edit Song Position
Shift T		Edit Tempo
I	I	Punch In on/off
O	O	Punch Out on/off
M	M	Master Tempo on/off
Z	Z	Auto Quantize on/off

PC	Mac	Function
Transport/Locators		
Page Down	Numlock	Rewind
Page Up	[Num] =	Forward
[Num] 0	[Num] 0	Stop
Space	Space	Alternate Stop Key
Enter	Enter	Start
0	0	Alternate Start Key
[Num] *	[Num] *	Record
9	9	Alternate Record Key
[Num] -	[Num] -	Tempo Down
[Num] +	[Num] +	Tempo Up
[Num] /	[Num] /	Cycle on/off
Alt [Num] 7	Option Home	Song Position to Selected Event
[Num] 1	[Num] 1	Position to Left Locator
Shift [Num] 1	Shift [Num] 1	Left Locator to Position
[Num] 2	[Num] 2	Position to Right Locator
Shift [Num] 2	Shift [Num] 2	Right Locator to Position
[Num] 7	Home	Editors: Position to Left of Window
Alt P	Option P	Locator to Selected Part(s)

Appendix 3
Instrument ranges

Use these as a guide when emulating real instruments with MIDI. These are safe, practical ranges, used when writing for real players. For a realistic interpretation avoid the high and low extremes except perhaps for solo passages.

Guitar E1 – E4

Bass Guitar E0 – G2

Trumpet E2 – Bb4

Trombone E1 – Bb3

Bass Trombone C1 – F3

Alto Saxophone Db2 – Ab4

Tenor Saxophone Ab1 – Eb4

Baritone Sax Db1 – Ab3

Soprano Sax Ab2 – Eb5

Flute C3 – C6

Piccolo D4 – Bb6

Oboe Bb2 – F5

Clarinet D2 – G5

Bassoon Bb0 – Bb3

French Horn B0 – F4

Violin G2 – C6

Viola C2 – C5

Cello C1 – G4

Double Bass E0 – G2

Harp Cb–1 – Gb6

Glockenspiel G4 – C7

Xylophone B3 – C6

Celesta C3 – C7

Marimba C2 – C6

Vibraphone F2 – F5

Index